Kingdom Identity

Lisa Ann

New Life Clarity Publishing
205 West 300 South, Brigham City, Utah 84302

Http://newlifeclarity.com/

Printed in the United States of America

ISBN- 979-8-2180-7799-0

Endorsements for *Kingdom Identity*

"It is with great joy that I recommend this book, "***Kingdom Identity***" for your library. This wonderful teaching/testimony of the author's journey of knowing Father God and then knowing herself through His eyes, will inspire you to believe only what God thinks of you, and reject every lie that your history seeks to define you. This book will raise your faith and confidence in God and His work in you.

Dr. Mike Hutchings
Director, Global Awakening School of Supernatural Ministry
President, God Heals PTSD Foundation.
https://www.godhealsptsd.com

"I'm loving this book! The readers will experience an understanding to unlock years of suffering and pain for people who will now begin to discover their identity."

Bishop Clinton Foster
Mentor, Founder
Bridge Ministry
www.faithbridges.org

In "**Kingdom Identity**" an entire lifetime of experiences are opened to the reader. For many, it will prove once again that the power of the Lord is as vast as it is mysterious. For others it will help connect "faith" with the term "Kingdom Identity". If you are not already on a path that brings you closer to walking in your identity as God's child, I hope this book causes you to think. For those of you that are already walking in your Kingdom Identity, I hope that this book will hasten your stride. Share this book with someone you know!

Knowing the author as I do, I can only confirm that this book was inspired by God and has been created with a purpose that I endorse. Keep writing Lisa Ann, this is good!

Ward E. Leber
Founder & Chairman
Child Safety Network™
www.CSN.org

Lisa Ann's book, **Kingdom Identity**, contains spiritual gems that will help you become all that God has designed you to be. Lisa shares her journey from brokenness to breakthrough through personal testimonies and the power of the word of God, bringing to life this necessary reality:

> *"And be not conformed to this world: but be ye transformed by the renewing of your mind, that ye may prove what [is] that good, and acceptable, and perfect, will of God." (Rom 12:2 KJV)*

If you desire more of God's life to be made known to and through you, this book will help you grow on your faith journey!

Alane Haynes
President and Co-Founder
Eternal Truth Now Ministry
http://alanehaynes.com/

"From the first day I met this woman of God, I saw in Lisa Ann a hunger for the truth of God's word. Her display of obedience is a quality I have rarely seen in anyone. Even before she knew what deliverance was, she was willing to trust God. She willingly said yes to Him without fear or embarrassment and stepped into her ***KINGDOM IDENTITY***. I am proud to call her my friend and sister in Christ. This book about Lisa's experiences will lead you through a journey of the ups and downs of life. The pages will illustrate to the reader how God never lets you go, no matter what; that He is ever present, even when you don't recognize it."

Anita Burton
Healing & Deliverance Minister
Speaking Life Ministry
www.SpeakingLifeMinistry.com

"Our Identity is at the core of who we believe we are. It directly affects our perception of God, others, and ourselves. Lisa Ann's new book, ***KINGDOM IDENTITY,*** inspires you to get past the superficial, as she candidly reveals her real-life stories and unveils the true meaning of living an authentic life of faith. A must read for anyone hungry to be all God has destined you to be!"

Maria Sainz
Senior Leader
Red Seal Ministries - San Diego, Ca.
www.redsealministries.com

"Lisa has put spiritual identity and purpose into terms that one can easily understand. With her story of addiction to living every day for God, we are able to relate to her story of overcoming adversity as it relates to the very essence of ***KINGDOM IDENTITY*** as those in faith." As Lisa models a transformed life she reflects the scripture found in John 1:12-13 "But as many received him, to them gave he power to become sons of God, even to them that believe on his name: which were born, not of blood, nor of the will of the flesh, nor of the will of man, but of God". Lisa is helping others to realize their new identity in Christ's KINGDOM IDENTITY.

"Well done!"
Deacon Will Rynerson
Director of Prison Ministry
Rock Church, San Diego, Ca.
www.sdrock.com/ministries/prison

"I'm privileged to endorse this powerful book by Lisa Ann. ***KINGDOM IDENTITY*** keeps you wanting more and will give hope to so many. It is evident that each page was written by the pen of her heart. Revelation 12:11-

"They overcame by the words of their testimony, to give others Hope."

Hope not in man but in the Creator of the universe, the Alpha and the Omega the Great I Am, by The Blood of King Jesus and power of the Holy Spirit. Lisa Ann is so real about sharing her life and transformation, that's what I love about her. She does not forget that it is from Gods mighty right hand that has brought her out of bondage.

She knows it takes work but also knows that it is worth knowing who you truly are, and why you were created. This book bears witness to your heart and soul that you're worthy, have a purpose, and most importantly who you are. Let this book encourage you to seek Him Jesus Christ and allow the Holy Spirit to walk you through your journey for His Glory. I can't wait to see what else Abba God has for Lisa Ann. God Bless You Woman of God. All Glory to God."

Pastor Mary Delozier
Founder
Open Door Ministry for The Broken - San Diego, Ca.
www.opendoorministryftb.org

"KINGDOM IDENTITY by Lisa Ann is an essential book to find the truth in knowing your identity. Choosing to believe lies over truth from life's challenges create struggles. Ephesians 6:12 "For our struggles are not against flesh and blood, but against the rulers, against the authorities, against the power of the dark world, the spiritual forces of evil in the heavenly realms. Lisa Ann's personal testimony of chasing the lies to fill the void in her heart, will bring revelation to know, if she can find the truth, so can we! I am blessed by her honesty! To seek a renewed mind in Christ brings hope and freedom!"

Dr. Michele Franklin
CEO & Founder
We Will Do It Together Ministries - San Diego, Ca.
www.wewilldoittogether.com

"Who am I?'" Is a profound introspective of the question that millions upon millions ask daily. People living in a mundane state of being draws on the propensity of society's consciousness to question the unknown mysteries from all social classes, who am I, and for what purpose was I put on earth? Those questions of one's identity in times of uncertainties can only be answered by the One who created us, God Almighty. If you want to know the purpose of a thing, you must first seek the Creator of that creation.

Lisa Ann's book ***Kingdom Identity*** does just that!

Humanity seeks their truth in others or material things that only gives a temporary moment of gratitude, but then become like all others, unfulfilling. This necessary book reveals the handwriting on the wall of the hearts of men and women who are desperately seeking the will and purpose for their lives. I endorse Lisa Ann and this masterfully etched work of art."

Ron Britton P.A.L.
Mentor & Founder
MegasAdelphos - San Diego, Ca.
www.MegasAdelphos.com

Dedication

I dedicate this book to the prodigals who have lost their way. If you have breath in your lungs, it's never too late to come home to the arms of the loving heavenly Father.

To those who have suffered at that hand of physical, sexual, emotional abuse, child abuse, domestic violence as the abused or the abuser, trauma, addiction, and any form of trafficking.

To all those who think they are alone and have been told they are a lost cause, you're not.

To the prisoner who wonders if freedom is available for them, it is.

To the misunderstood, misguided, misfits. God loves you & so do I!

To my mom for always praying for me. To my sister and brother for seeing the best in me.

And most of all to my daughter; you are my precious gift, blessed beyond measure - I love you!

Acknowledgements

Thank You God,

It's truly an honor and privilege to share hope with the world and invite people to be set free in Christ. *All* things are possible through your grace and mercy when we believe. Cover me under The Shadow of Your Wings, make me invisible so that when people read this book or meet me, they will have a hunger for Your righteousness. I pray that every nation in the world knows the love of a Heavenly Father who makes beauty from ashes, no one is forgotten.

Amen

...

Thank you to all who have spoken into my life and destiny, who are praying for my continued journey and transformation process. I honor and appreciate you beyond words! When you feel like you're at the end of your rope, tie a knot and hang on. Not one of us has it all together and none of us are perfect but we can do All things through Christ who gives us strength!

All praise and thanks be to God for calling me out of the grave to be a witness of His love and mercy.

Table of Contents

Introduction

I was born on a Navy Base in Newport Rhode Island. My father was a Roman Catholic Italian from Brooklyn, New York. My mom migrated to Queens NY from Edinburgh, Scotland when she was 16 years old. At the age of 18 she married her brother's best friend, my dad. I'm a 3rd generation American on my fathers side, and 1st generation American on my mother's side.

I was raised Roman Catholic, baptized when I was less than a year old and received the first holy communion at age 5. I attended Catechism (CCD), made my sacrament of confirmation at the age of 8 and took on my grandmother's name Eva. (Confirmation is the sacrament by which Catholics receive a special outpouring of the Holy Spirit). I had no idea what was going on but did as I was told as a child.

At the age of 13, my mom took me to a Pentecostal church, and I willingly gave my life to Christ there. But immediately after, I was led into the dark side of life and struggled from a battle within. I ran away from home at a very young age. I got tangled up with some bad people and was involved in things that should have killed me or made me lose my mind. I wandered lost for 22 years.

In 2003 I was arrested and sentenced to 10 years. I filed an appeal, acquired time off for a drug program, and good behavior. When my appeal was granted I received time served and was immediately released in February 2008! As I look back it was a blessing. I know it was God's saving grace and I don't look at it as an arrest, I was rescued. A few years after being released from prison, I moved to CA in 2011 and began attending the Rock Church in Point Loma, CA.

In 2013 I began attending a Thursday morning women's bible study at C3 Church on Balboa (now Awaken San Diego) where I met a woman named Anita. One day she invited me to lunch with a group of women after the bible study but as I was going to leave the church parking lot, I decided not to go. However, while I was waiting for the light to turn green, instead of my car turning left, it seemed as if my car lifted off the ground and went straight into the parking lot across the street which was the restaurant parking lot. I said to myself, "Well, I guess I'm going to lunch!"

When I walked into the restaurant, the ladies welcomed me with open arms. Anita was looking at me intensely and I could see it in her eyes that she was seeing something in the spirit.

She asked me if she could pray for me and I questioned, "Right here in the restaurant with all these people?"

"Yes of course," she said, "They probably want a prayer too!"

I laughed and reluctantly said yes. What commenced was a prayer that I never knew existed and I received an encounter that totally changed the way I saw what I then knew to be religion.

Before she began to pray, she told me to cross my wrists over each other like an 'X'. Very calmly and confidently, she looked me in the eye and said, "I'm going to pray for you now."

She told me, "When I say break the chains, I want you to imagine those chains breaking off your wrists. So, when I say that you break the chains off and physically make the motion of separating your wrists, ok?"

I didn't hesitate or question it for a second. I just said OK. When Anita prayed for me and came to the part about breaking the chains in Jesus' name, she said, "Ok, do it now!"

I broke my hands apart and I immediately felt something let go of my wrists but felt shackles clamp around my ankles! This is when I knew spiritual warfare was real! I began to stomp my feet and say "My ankles! Something clamped around my ankles!"

At this point I no longer cared that we were in a restaurant nor who was watching. I wanted to be free no matter what.

Anita is a Kingdom Warrior, she didn't stop there, she literally got under the table, pointed her finger at my ankles and said, "I command you to let go of her and get out of here right now in Jesus' name."

I felt the pressure let go of my ankles, the shackles fell off and I felt an overwhelming sense of peace that I have never felt before. I felt like I was no longer sitting in the booth at the restaurant, it was as if I was floating.

This freedom session pointed me in the direction of wanting to know more about what is available to us through Jesus. It ignited a hunger in me to learn more about my identity as a child of God, and what this spiritual warfare was all about.

I started serving on the SD Rock Church Bon-Fire Ministry team as a hostess. We met for a bonfire, worship music, and prayer on the bay two times a month during the summer.

At this time, I was still attending the women's Thursday morning bible study at C3 and made a decision to get baptized in water at their Sunday service. I wanted more of what I saw God was doing in other people, I wanted to be set on fire. I signed up for and was baptized in water and filled with the gift of the Holy Spirit at C3 Church in 2014. When I went under the water, I felt the grime and residue of my past wash off and I was cleansed in spirit. As I emerged from under the water, It felt like I was shedding my old skin.

I was born anew

I joined the Prison Ministry at the City Heights location of the Rock Church in 2015 and joined the Altar call team shortly thereafter for about 3 years. Praying for others and knowing what God brought me out of; gave me a burning desire to see others get set free! I began to partner with organizations, ministries, safe houses, rehabs, transitional homes to share hope with those in residency. Because of these experiences, I knew I couldn't go back to religion and simply just show up for church to serve on Sundays.

We all are important in God's Kingdom, all of us have an assignment, purpose, and destiny. Until my last breath I will share the Good News of who Jesus is and what God has done in my life. I know the power of being in relationship with our creator, the One True Living God. You too can experience the best relationship of your life, live in authority by knowing your kingdom identity and step into your destiny!

Numbers 6:24-26 NIV- "*The Lord bless you and keep you; the Lord make his face shine on you and be gracious to you; the Lord turn his face toward you and give you peace.*"

About the Author

Lisa Ann is a business owner, and the founder of '*Hearts On Fire-Ministries*'. She has the heart of an Evangelist and wants to see everyone set free. Kingdom Identity was written to bring hope and share an outpouring of love from a living God. She has spent the last five years taking trauma-informed classes to acquire tools to help those who have gone through severe traumatic experiences, as well as help others become more trauma-informed.

After overcoming her own history of child abuse and exploitation, Lisa Ann founded '*Hearts On Fire-Ministries*' in 2017 and partners with other ministries, outreaches and churches for fellowship, live worship music on the bay in San Diego, teachings, conferences, outreach, healing and deliverance. We are called to share the Good News of the gospel, and love like Jesus.

Lisa Ann met Dr. Mike Hutchings who is the Director of Dr. Randy Clark Global Awakening Ministries at a PTSD seminar for war veterans In 2018. It was then she learned that Post Traumatic Stress Disorder was not only for veterans. Anyone who has experienced trauma can suffer its effects. She is a year 1 graduate of Dr. Randy Clark- Global Awakening's Supernatural Ministry – School of Healing and Deliverance. After many of her own inner healing and deliverance sessions, Lisa Ann completed a training seminar with '*I-Connect Up Inner Healing and Deliverance*' with Katie & Mitch Luse. Lisa Ann continues learning about the supernatural abundant life from respected Holy Spirit filled mentors.

The following year, she began attending biblical seminary at San Diego's School of Theology and then in 2019 began preaching the Gospel at San Diego Living Water Church. Lisa has led thousands of people to salvation, freedom and deliverance through prayer. *Hearts On Fire- Ministries* has broadcasted "The Truth on Thursdays" through live stream channels on Facebook and YouTube. She has partnered with other leaders through Zoom sessions to pray for and minister to church leaders of Vietnam, as well as host healing and deliverance training for men and women in Pakistan through a live translator of their native language.

Lisa Ann sits on the advisory panel of the Child Safety Network since 2019 as a Human Trafficking expert. Aside from her work with the Child Safety Network, Lisa Ann ministers to people from all walks of life so that they can be free in Christ, grab hold of their Kingdom Identity, step into their destiny and then help others find freedom.

Lisa Ann has volunteered with Generate Hope Safe House for Trafficked Women, San Diego Dream Center for Outreach to the homeless. She has preached at rallys such as the Center for Justice and Reconciliation with Point Loma Nazarene, "CAT" (Churches Against Trafficking) "KNOW MORE" in partnership with Petals ministry at the Rock Church; to bring awareness to counselors, case workers, task force, and teachers on the signs of domestic abuse and trafficking victims. Lisa Ann partners with the Freedom Center in San Diego and undercover task forces in the project to end human trafficking.

Lisa Ann lives in San Diego, Ca. with her dog Halo.

Request an Emotional Healing and Deliverance Session Via ZOOM

info@heartsonfire-ministries.com

About Hearts On Fire- Ministries

Hearts On Fire- Ministries provides training, resources, education, and awareness to equip and restore the lives of those who have been impacted by human trafficking, domestic violence, homelessness, addiction and child abuse.

The ministry provides resources and teachings including print, audio, video, social media and live events to equip, and educate all walks of life. We partner with other ministries, and churches to provide resources, materials, and finances to restore lives.

No one is overlooked, we reach out to people of all ages and in all walks of life. Hearts On Fire- Ministries is built on a foundation of faith, integrity and dedicated volunteer partners and supporters who share this call.

The belief and core value of this ministry is that all can be set free, and that God provides healing and full restoration to all impacted by traumatic experiences. Our mission is to encourage and equip people to be healed, made whole, and then serve others in need around them.

Stay Connected!

Hearts On Fire-Ministries
Lisa Ann- Founder, Mentor
Email: *info@heartsonfire-ministries.com*
Facebook: *https://www.facebook.com/sdheartsonfire*

YouTube: *https://www.youtube.com/c/LisaAnnHeartsOnFire*
Instagram: *https://www.instagram.com/sdheartsonfireministries*
Website: *www.heartsonfire-ministries.com*

Chapter 1

Who Am I?

People have spent their entire lives searching for themselves.

Who am I?

What is my purpose?

Identity formation can be impacted by so many things- family, ethnicity, race, culture, location, opportunities, media, interests, appearance, self-expression, and life experiences. Life is full of opportunities and choices, but if we don't know our identity and purpose, we could end up on a life path that we aren't built for. Your identity is found in knowing to whom you belong. Your sphere of kingdom influence begins by knowing who you are, and *you* are a child of the *King*.

God loves you just as you are, but He wants you to be free in your Kingdom Identity and live life to the fullest.

We are human, and as humans we will never get it right while on this Earth! Adam and Eve removed perfection from our human abilities in the garden.

We will mess up- it is our nature, but God will put us in a position to use our setbacks as a testimony to help someone else. God *knows* your heart and loves you even in your imperfection. Kingdom Identity is an ever-changing and transforming journey that *glorifies* God along the way. Since stepping into my Kingdom Identity as a daughter of the *King*, I do my best to make healthy choices that will please God.

Making healthy decisions begins with the renewal of our minds, in order to ensure our emotions don't sway us. Included in this process, God transforms our character to be bold, yet kind. He wants to transform your character, renew your mind, and give you a different perspective on how you see others and yourself.

We all have our ups and downs in life. It's what we do in those times that will make or break us. God has protected me through self-destructive behaviors that put me around influences and placed me in situations that should have killed me. I've made some tremendously foolish and dangerous decisions, throwing caution to the wind; I didn't know who I was. My *true* identity had been lost.

And as I reflect on my past, it has become clear that the things of the world and the devil's lies clouded my mind and *stole* my identity. I thought I had it together and believed I was in full control. That was the farthest thing from the truth!

But what we fail to see is that we don't know what *freedom* looks like when all we know is *bondage.*

Unknowingly, I was swept along by the father of lies. It was rooted in what others told me about myself. It resulted from me trying to live up to a false identity and keep up a facade trying to impress others.

Not knowing who I was, opened the door to a cycle of misconceptions and confusion. I was trying to please others, but I lost *myself* in the process.

The Battle Within

There is a spiritual war taking place. The angels of darkness and the angels of light are in a battle for our very souls. The battlefield begins in our minds. The battle within our mind is the fiercest battle that we shall ever face.

Thank you for joining me as I share what I've learned about the struggle we all face in order to find our Kingdom Identity. I began my journey of transformation after getting baptized in water and spirit in 2014, and I will continue to share what God has done until my last breath.

My mom had me when she was just 18 years old and did the best she could. I was a junior high school dropout and runaway. That led me into a life of crime and addiction. From the age of 13, I believed I was destined to be a career criminal. Abused as a child, the pain in my heart was more than I could bear. I didn't want to confront it because the hurt was unbearable, I was in pain, and pain seeks pleasure. My heart was empty-something was missing, and so I searched outward.

I looked to the wrong people for validation and cocaine became my closest friend. I was a vulnerable target to the lies of the enemy. Satan moved right in with his mind manipulation and deception—he took advantage of my weakness. I wanted the same things everyone else does- to be liked and accepted. I had no idea where I belonged or how I fit in. I searched for places, people, and things to fill the void. Always running from myself, yet everywhere I went, I was always alone.

For over 22 years, I wandered in the darkness. I stayed lost for a long time because I believed in a lie from the pit of hell. I had no idea who I was, and in my mind, I thought the way I was living was the only way I could live. I was trapped in a lie. I became a puppet on the enemy's stage. It may begin subtly, yet when you are sucked in; you suddenly wake up one day to find yourself weaved into a web of lies and deception.

In 2003, I hit rock bottom. I fell to my knees when facing 25 years to life in federal prison. I was sentenced to 10 years. An Angel of hope came to visit me and told me to go to the law library and file an appeal, so I did.

I believed that God was calling me near to Him and told me that one day I would get immediate release. I stood in faith, and God met me right where I was, alone and broken.

Then suddenly it *happened*!

Almost 6 years into a 10-year sentence, my appeal was approved and with time off for good behavior and completing a drug program - I was granted immediate release.

I share this because I know what it is to be lost. Have you ever felt so lost you didn't know who you are? I believe we all experience that feeling at one point or another in our lives. It's not easy, but God can do His most extraordinary work through our brokenness. Today I don't question my identity. I know who I am and who I belong to. I am a child of God. God knew us before we were formed in our mother's womb. Our Kingdom Identity begins with knowing who we are as His child.

I am who He says I am. I am His, and so are *you*!

He has created all of us for greatness! Everything I was looking for was inside of me the entire time. And it's inside of you as well; there is greatness in there!

Being strong-willed will only get us so far. Willpower only produces short-term change. Therefore, we must allow God to change the way we think. Everything we do begins with a thought. Every behavior is motivated by a belief, and every action is a result of our attitude.

Insecurities take root in our lives and show up as masks in the form of offense and denial. We often dress up the outside with clothes and material things to cover up the hurt of what is inside. When we don't know who we are, the devil builds a prison in our minds and does everything he can to torment us and keep us trapped. God wants us to live free and He frees us by knowing ourselves through Him. I am not saying that I don't have challenging moments, I am sure we all do. But today I do my best to stay aware of the battle in my mind.

Be Transformed by The Renewing of Your Mind

> Romans 12:2 NIV- *"Do not conform to the pattern of this world but be transformed by the renewing of your mind. Then you will be able to test and approve what God's will is, his good, pleasing, and perfect will."*

Through the renewal of our minds, we begin to recognize the temptations and the triggers that will take us out of the place God has called us to go. He has a special calling for your life. I believe your reading of this book is not a coincidence. Allow God to transform your mind and believe in who He says you are. You are a Kingdom warrior beloved.

You are crowned as royalty through your Kingdom identity; believe it and step into your destiny.

> Isaiah 44:22 NLT- *"I have swept away your sins like a cloud. I have scattered your offenses like the morning mist. Oh, return to me, for I have paid the price to set you free."*

God wrapped Himself in the flesh, came to earth in human form as Jesus and paid the price of death for our sin past and present. So, leave the lies of shame and guilt at the cross where Jesus died for you.

The Bible tells us to take every thought captive. I encourage you to let this Scripture take root within you.

> 2 Corinthians 10:5 NIV- *"We demolish arguments and every pretension that sets itself up against the knowledge of God, and we take captive every thought to make it obedient to Christ."*

This is a command- not a suggestion. We seek God's will for our lives and not to gratify the flesh's sinful desires. The things of this world we previously sought for gratification, we no longer find pleasure in.

As we put on the new self, we hunger and thirst for His righteousness. Reject negativity and allow calmness, peace, and joy to flow in you and through you.

Our hearts and minds live very close to one another in our bodies. If they are not in communication and aligned, they can be worlds apart. That's a dangerous place to be. Instead of reacting to what once triggered you, you will begin taking your thoughts captive and find yourself responding in love. By reading the Bible you will find clarity and alignment of the head and heart. Test your thoughts. Are they pure? Are they full of love? Are they from a place of power and sound mind in Christ? Do they line up with scripture and what God says about you?

Over time, we learn to recognize three different thoughts or voices in our minds: our own, those from the devil, and those from God. Many of us may not have grown up with positive affirmations.

You may have been told negative things about yourself by your parents, teachers, family members. Unfortunately, the negative words that we grow up with become our beliefs about ourselves. It's vital to be careful of who we surround ourselves with, who we allow to speak into us, and what we believe about ourselves. Everything we expose ourselves to goes into the mind and can either contaminate or flourish our thoughts.

In Isaiah 43:1 NIV the Bible tells us - *"Do not fear, for I have redeemed you; I have summoned you by name; you are mine."*

Redeemed means to gain or regain possession of (something) in exchange for payment. His blood has purchased you. The redemption word group refers to both deliverance from sin and freedom from captivity in the New Testament.

Jesus redeemed you, and this means he paid a dear price for you- His life! His blood is a deposit of our inheritance in Heaven. No matter where you've been or what you've done, He purchased you with His bloodshed on the cross because He loves you!

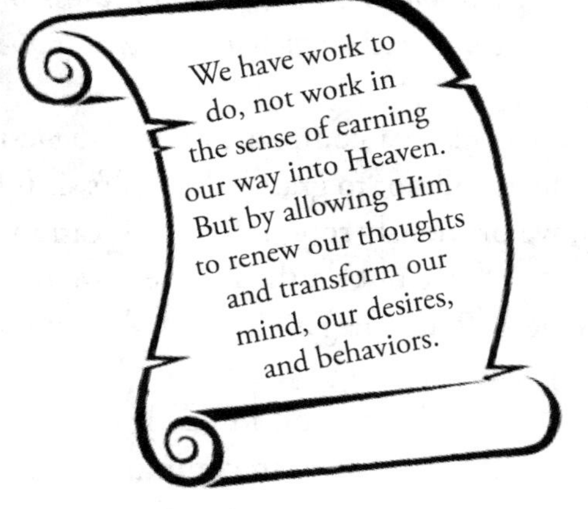

When you accept Christ as your savior and believe in your heart that He was crucified, went to hell, and took back the keys from satan then rose from the dead on the third day to save you, you gain freedom. You are now free from the chains and bondage of both slavery to *sin* and its *guilt*.

But it doesn't end there.

We have work to do, not work in the sense of earning our way into Heaven. But by allowing Him to renew our thoughts and transform our mind, our desires, and behaviors. God places our character on His potter's wheel!

Through His unfailing, never-ending love, He transforms us from the inside out. He loves us despite all the things we have or haven't done. We could never *earn* His love and He doesn't want us to try to. We've all sinned and done something we're ashamed to admit. You are precious in God's eyes; leave your past at the cross where Jesus took on all our sins. He did it for you and for me.

Are you willing to come as you are and watch what He does in your life? Then, get ready to step into a transformation that no person, drink, drug, or pill could ever do. I am a living witness to what only Jesus can do when we believe.

You are *worthy*. You are *loved*. You are *chosen*.

You are cherished!

You Are an Overcomer in Christ.

As we read the Word of God, our faith grows, and we overcome obstacles and challenges that used to hinder us. When we apply God's word to our daily lives, our minds are renewed, and God transforms us from the inside out. God wants us to be happy, joyous, free, and aligned with His will for our lives.

> 2 Timothy 1:7 NKJV- *"For God has not given us a spirit of fear but of power and love and a sound mind."*

We will never be perfect as humans, and our works won't get us into heaven. But, when God looks at us, He sees through the lens of love and sees us as His children. Because of the blood Jesus shed on the cross, we are perfect in Christ, it makes us clean in God's eyes. That's the power of the blood of Christ. Our sins are washed away; we are white as snow, brand new.

At the time of salvation, we are forgiven and made whole in Christ. Our sins have been washed away by the power of the blood of The Lamb. When Jesus died- He died for us, and when He rose, we were resurrected with Him.

When we trust Him and seek His will as children of God, we are transformed, and our minds are renewed. No matter how many times we fall, His mercies are renewed every morning. Walking in love with the power of the Holy Spirit alive in us gives us a desire to want to do better, not only for ourselves but also to help others.

The transformation of our minds in Christ brings us peace. The torment that once held our minds in bondage is transformed into peace no matter what our circumstances.

You are worthy of good things, and God loves you. You are His favorite; He made you perfect in His sight, and you are essential to what He is doing on this earth. God chose you before the beginning of time. Focus on things that are good, beautiful, and true. Speak of good things for your life, encourage yourself and others. What you think about it will keep growing. Just because we have a terrible day doesn't mean we have a horrible life. Speak to your future and believe in the goodness of God for your life. No matter what your past or your current situation may be, keep your eyes fixed on Jesus, and you will see what's on the other side of those mountains.

What we think about ourselves is crucial to who we are becoming. Taking thoughts captive means that I have a chance to do something about all the thoughts and ideas that are not well-pleasing to my life. We have the power to take every thought captive to be obedient to what God thinks about us before they enter our hearts and minds and become a part of what we believe. Scientists don't agree on how many thoughts we have each day, but all agree there are at least thousands of them. Our identity is shaped by every moment of our lives and by the influences we allow into our minds. These transform into thoughts that essentially become our beliefs and how we view ourselves. Capture and test your every thought. Does it come from God or the enemy? Is it your own thoughts? Do they align with what the Bible says?

When we are aware, we can test the spirits. Ask yourself, are these thoughts disruptive, or are they constructive? It's about consciously deciding to be aware and allowing this cleansing transformation shift to take place by renewing our minds. This cleansing comes from washing ourselves in the water of the Word. For example, reading the Bible will cleanse your mind from the lies of the devil and the world. This is part of cultivating your beliefs into the truth of who God says you are.

Don't be hard on yourself. Life is a *journey*, not a *race*. It unfolds minute by minute, day by day. Transformation is a lifelong process.

We are constantly building new memories over our old ones. The lies that once choked us are being chopped off at the roots. Allow the word of God to open your spiritual ears and eyes. Focus your thoughts, decision-making process, and ideas on being aligned to the Word of God. I pray for your spiritual eyes to be opened to recognizing and rejecting dangerous traps from the devil. You are what you think. What you thought yesterday has brought you where you are today, and what you believe today will take you where you are going tomorrow.

We can find peace when we live our lives focused on positive thoughts and cast out the negative ones. Be alert and of a sober mind. The devil prowls around like a lion seeking someone to devour. Pay attention to triggers and traps of the enemy. You have control over your thoughts and how you respond to the world around you. Before you react, analyze the situation or information that is in front of you. When we pause and seek to identify a situation as Jesus would see it, we can control our thoughts, and we don't allow our emotions to rule us. No one said it was easy; it's so much easier said than done! Taking your thoughts captive is like training a muscle, the more we exercise the stronger we become.

Transformation of our mind begins with inner emotional healing and letting go of past hurts. We all are a work in progress. God wants us better, not bitter. He wants to live inside of you. God while still in heaven, came to earth as Jesus, and left us with the gift of the Holy Spirit, God is all three in one! I encourage you to let the Holy Spirit guide you.

Our mind controls our thoughts, our thoughts become our attitudes, which, in turn, influence our behaviors and develop our character. Identify your feelings and listen to the voice of truth within. When we capture positive thoughts, peace and joy become our portion, and we can walk in a well-rounded life.

The Holy Spirit is our comforter and wants to guide you and fill you with His Dunamis (power and abilities). With guidance from the Holy Spirit, we become one with the Father, and He protects and guides our footsteps.

This does not mean there won't be any problems or situations in our lives. Remember, we live in the world even though we are not *of this world*. But it does mean that we will be able to endure times of hardship and suffering when we face our fears head-on and view situations from a transformed mind allowing faith to be our loudest voice. Our strength and help come from the Lord.

When we seek guidance from God and look to Him for advice, He draws near to us. When we trust in Him, we will continually walk with increased peace, power, love, and sound mind no matter what we are going through. God loves us unconditionally. No matter what we've done or how many times we have turned our back on His love, He is there waiting for us. He is a Good Father always ready to shower us with His love and offers us comfort and safety in His arms. No matter what we may be going through, when we look to the Word of God, we find answers. When we seek Him in faith, He guides us to good things throughout our life.

We are unshakeable when standing on His Word, believing His promises, and wearing The Armor of God.

The Armor of God

Ephesians 6:10-17 NIV-

"10 Finally, be strong in the Lord and in his mighty power.

11 Put on the full armor of God, so that you can take your stand against the devil's schemes.

12 For our struggle is not against flesh and blood, but against the rulers, against the authorities, against the powers of this dark world and against the spiritual forces of evil in the heavenly realms.

13 Therefore put on the full armor of God, so that when the day of evil comes, you may be able to stand your ground, and after you have done everything, to stand.

14 Stand firm then, with the belt of truth buckled around your waist, with the breastplate of righteousness in place,

15 and with your feet fitted with the readiness that comes from the gospel of peace.

16 In addition to all this, take up the shield of faith, with which you can extinguish all the flaming arrows of the evil one.

17 Take the helmet of salvation and the sword of the Spirit, which is the word of God."

By covering ourselves in the armor of God, we are shielded with His protection; we are equipped to discern and defend ourselves from the tricks and temptations the devil sends our way to distract and trap us. Reading your Bible, learning His Word, memorizing verses, and speaking them from your mouth will restore your soul. The Kingdom of God is voice-activated, open your mouth and declare God's promises over your life, your family, your children, and their children's children. Write scriptures down and consider sticking them on your mirrors until they take root in your soul, heck I even put my favorite one in my shoe!

Dressed in His armor daily, we are prepared to enter the world and overcome any situations that may come against us. The devil is tricky and uses manipulation, lies, and deceit to take you out of your Godly character. Sometimes, the devil will try to use what we see to trick us and throw us off what God has planned for us. Without the Word of God and the armor of God, we are vulnerable to attacks from the devil and all the things life throws at us. We will never get it all right, and we are not perfect, but by staying covered in the armor, we will be able to bind up fear, stress, anxiety, anger, frustration, just to name a few soul-stealing tactics the devil uses to throw us off. God's armor gives us the power to overcome these forms of attack and covers us with His peace and blessed assurance in times of trouble. Pray your way into each day in confidence as you wrap yourself in God's armor. Thank You, God, for supplying us with Your armor to protect us.

God's desire for us is to be aware of who we are, and the Bible offers us the tools for battle and teaches us how to recognize the enemy's schemes, lies, and tactics. The armor of God represents the defense we must take in our spiritual lives. The Bible tells us that we are fighting a war against satan, the manipulator who seeks to destroy us. Therefore, we must defend ourselves and put on God's armor. As Christians, it is important for us to understand the severity of this battle, the devil is a liar and a thief.

> John 10:10 ESV- *"The thief comes only to steal and kill and destroy. I came that they may have life and have it abundantly."*

The enemy has robbed us of *more* than enough! But, through Christ Jesus, God will give us back what the devil has stolen!

> Joel 2:25-27 NIV- *"I will repay you for the years the locusts have eaten— the great locust and the young locust, the other locusts and the locust swarm— my great army that I sent among you. You will have plenty to eat until you are full, and you will praise the name of the LORD your God, who has worked wonders for you; never again will my people be shamed. Then you will know that I am in Israel, that I am the LORD your God, and that there is no other; never again will my people be shamed."*

Invite Him into Your Life

God is not a thief; He will not sneak into your life to bring you peace, love, and joy. We must ask Him for it. When we do, the transformation begins, and there is a never-ending love from God that we receive. He loves us beyond measure. It is *indescribable.*

It's time to reset your mindset. It takes work. I had been in and out of counseling and therapy my entire life battling depression, anxiety, addiction, anger, and fear. I was diagnosed with depression, PTSD, bipolar, and ADHD. Lies, bitterness and confusion distorted the lens I used to see myself through. I was broken, lost, confused, and afraid. The truth of the Gospel set me free by the blood of Jesus Christ. Freedom came through seeking the love of our precious Lord and Savior.

God can, does, and will take the broken things in our life and turn them around to be used to help someone else for His glory. So, step out in faith and believe that He sees you.

I didn't know that the struggles and trauma I experienced, God would someday use to help others who may be going through or have gone through something similar. When the renewing of our mind transforms us, we see things in a way that pleases God.

Transformation of our minds helps us to see others as Jesus does. He gives us a new way of thinking, the way we view ourselves and the world around us.

I have a true passion and desire to help people. Seeing the pain and suffering of others breaks my heart. Kingdom Identity is knowing your authority in Christ to stomp out the devil and crush the lies by sharing hope and love with others through the power of your testimony.

> Revelation 12:11 KJV- "*And they overcame him by the blood of the Lamb and by the word of their testimony.*"

God has shown up so many times in my life, I should have been dead or lost my mind. No one can tell me He's not real; I'm a living witness!

Sharing hope with others through your life's experiences may be exactly what they have been waiting for. There are souls assigned to you. Perhaps sharing your hope will open the door to their freedom. The Holy Spirit will ignite in you a passion for others and transform you to see others through the eyes of Jesus. Your transformation will give you the heart of Christ, and you will desire to do the same and help someone else. I know God has had His arms around me through every step and every breath on my path of self-destruction.

Ephesians 2:10 NIV- "*For we are God's handiwork, created in Christ Jesus to do good works, which God prepared in advance for us to do.*"

Delivered from old habits, from darkness into light, He has prepared us in advance for where we find ourselves today. There is a transformation and renewing of the mind that occurs when you decide to follow Christ.

God wants you to be happy. His guidance and instruction are in His Word. There will be good and bad circumstances throughout life. But, with the Lord as your shepherd, He will lead you beside quiet waters regardless of the circumstances; things will turn around if you just believe and let faith be your loudest voice.

Throughout life, we go through trials and tests. God does not cause bad things in our life, nor does He want us to hurt. Sometimes He allows us to walk through the valley of the shadow of death and uses these trials to make us stronger and wiser. But God protects us through the darkness. He also allows us to struggle to the point of surrender to Him. He gives us thicker skin and we come out of our experiences more knowledgeable than we were before. If He gave us everything we wanted when we wanted it, we wouldn't need Him. He stretches us in times of our brokenness, and continually transforms us. He wants us to look to Him through all times, good and bad. You are His own, and He knows you by name; you are His Beloved. What an honor and privilege it is to be selected and set apart for His Great works. Never stop seeking Him. We are unshakable through all circumstances when we remain steadfast in Christ Jesus.

We are engaged in a spiritual war. Negative thoughts are from the enemy, and we are fighting on a battlefield in our minds. It is satans ultimate pleasure to distract us, and throw us off course and to convince us that we are weak. Yet when we resist temptations, God is faithful and always gives us a way out. Every day when you wake up, ask the Holy Spirit to fill your heart and mind. Start off your day with praise and worship.

James 4:7 ESV- *Submit yourselves therefore to God. Resist the devil, and he will flee from you.*

Prayer- *"Lord, thank you for filling me with a heart like Jesus. Lord, teach me to love those around me. Thank You for using me as a vessel for Your love and light to shine into the world."*

God Wants Us to Be Aware and Discerning

Matthew 10:16 ESV- *"Behold, I send you out as sheep in the midst of wolves. Therefore, be wise as serpents and harmless as doves."*

When we are aware, we learn to recognize the enemy's tactics and notice that he wants to distract from what God has for us. That's the devil's job, to steal everything that God has for us.

With the renewing of our minds, we will be equipped to avoid getting sucked in and consumed by trials of what we may know as familiar.

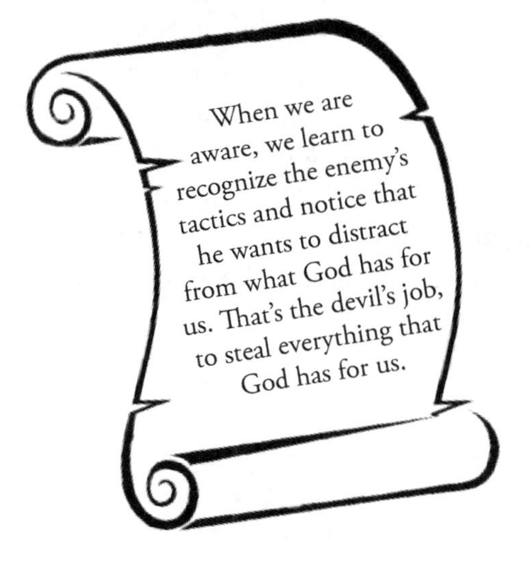

We have authority in Christ to change those cycles. Break the chains! We are children of God Almighty maker of Heavens and the Earth, we are redeemed and set free by the blood of Christ. No longer slaves!

Re-train your brain and ask God to give you discernment to recognize the enemy's schemes and tactics. Our eyes and ears are our gates to the mind. Be careful what you open your gates to and what you allow to enter your gates. The word of God is alive and in you and in me. He transforms and renews our minds and our thinking. Set free and made whole, in Christ!

The Holy Spirit is alive in us. When our spirit is submitted to the guidance of the Holy Spirit, and we are fueled by consuming the Word of God, our Kingdom Identity journey begins. God disciplines us for our good. Sometimes digging up the worms and pulling roots and skeletons out of the closet can be painful. However, once we learn to take thoughts captive, our stinking thinking transforms, we develop new habits and new healthy ways of thinking. When ideas come into our minds, we learn to take every thought captive to be obedient in Christ, recognize where they are coming from, and analyze our next move, purposeful and strategic, from a Kingdom Mindset.

When you embrace God's will for your life and walk in humility, you will want to make better decisions that please God. Then, peace will surround your life no matter what you face. We are all on a journey- but knowing our Kingdom Identity transforms our minds!

Act, move your feet, and participate. The Word of God lays a foundation, then builds a house of His love within us. Capturing every thought and aligning it with who He says we are comes from studying what He says about us as His children in the Bible.

By applying His Word to our lives, we receive strength, our minds are transformed, and we walk in authority through Christ and our Kingdom Identity becomes a lifestyle.

Chapter 2
Radical Faith

2 Corinthians 5:7 NIV- *"For we live by faith not by sight."*

The revelation of God's glory is being poured out on the earth, people are hungry for answers like never before, and the seeker-sensitive church is fading. Unfortunately, people seek psychics and witch doctors for answers before seeking healing and deliverance from God because of the lack of authoritative power displayed by most believers today. God wants us to be healed, happy and whole.

The Word of God is His divine instruction and guidance for our lives, His promises written in the scriptures are to build up our faith. When you read the Word of God, it settles into your heart and ignites a fire. When we believe in His promises, trust His goodness, and speak it out loud from our mouth in faith, it activates blessings. Faith comes by hearing and hearing comes by the Word of God.

Everyone Has Needs, But Not Everyone Has Faith

So, when we step out in faith, we are empowered to accomplish all that God has for our lives. God does and will speak to us today through His Word, dreams, visions, and various limitless ways. If you're seeking to hear from Him, you will!

Radical faith is trusting and believing that God can bring your vision to life; and make your dreams a reality. Faith is an action word; we must actively move into what we believe to be true no matter what it looks like in the natural world. Without faith no one can please God. Anyone who comes to God must believe that He is real and that He rewards those who truly want to find Him.

My very first aspiration that made any sense was to be free! I wanted to be set free from the bondage of sadness, anger, insecurity, addiction, anxiety and more. Once I stepped out in faith, my freedom journey began. I made a heartfelt decision to seek Jesus Christ. Nothing else ever worked but I knew God had saved me from the pit of hell, brought me out of the darkness, even raised me from the dead; and there had to be a reason for it. He has a plan for our lives, but it is the devil's mission to keep us from reaching our God-assigned destiny.

I had faith and believed that God had a purpose for my life and that His love for me was far greater than what I thought about myself and the way I was living. Unfortunately, like many of us, I had put my trust and faith in all the wrong people and things, but it taught me valuable lessons.

Faith is our absolute trust in God's love for us, regardless of our circumstances. God does have a purpose and plan for our lives. Believing in what we can't see and allowing faith to be our loudest voice unlocks doors as we step into our assigned Kingdom purpose.

True faith in God, especially through trials, is trusting and believing that He is working everything out for our best interest.

I'm not talking about an occupation; I'm talking about a *God-given purpose.* I believe our primary purpose in life is to have a relationship with God first and then with others. No matter what is going on in your life, faith means putting complete trust or confidence in God for the best outcome no matter what you are experiencing now. True faith in God, especially through trials, is trusting and believing that He is working everything out for our best interest.

We need to make a conscious choice and effort in faith to seek the voice of God and ask Him to reveal our assigned gifts. We are all different parts of one body, each part needed by one and another to function properly. According to the Scriptures, these gifts include such ministries as faith, healing, prophecy, proclamation, teaching, administration, reconciliation, compassion, and self-sacrificing service and charity for the help and encouragement of people. It takes all kinds of different gifts and talents, but we are all essential. Whatever you do, do it with excellence unto the Lord, and you will prosper. This does not mean you won't have troubles or hard times because they will come! Our faith that God will make a way is the strength that sustains us.

Faith is based on the belief that we have a Divine Creator who is the maker of all things and that He loves us. We understand that our Creator God is a good Father who loves us unconditionally and who wants to protect, guide, and help His children. And like a good parent, He would never harm us and only wants what is best for us. When our faith is strong, we have absolute trust in God's love for us, regardless of our circumstances, and look to Him for guidance.

Faith requires us to understand and accept God's expectations for us, taught to us by Jesus. God wants us to love others with a heart of genuine, sincere kindness and compassion. This means that we are to be humble, not thinking too highly of ourselves. We ought not be critical or judgmental, hurtful or take advantage of others. Instead, we help those who need help. And when we are wronged, we will forgive just as we are forgiven, by grace.

If we love God, we will also love people. Constantly. Not just to those we like or are close to us like family and friends, but everyone. When we stumble, we can ask God for forgiveness, and we too, will be forgiven.

Faith reminds us that God wants us to join Him in heaven, but our hearts must reflect God's love. We show our hearts with our thoughts, how we speak to others, how we treat others, and how we live our lives. It is important to understand that those who do not accept God and our love for Him are still watching our actions, and we want to represent God well every day, not just on Sundays.

Faith will compel us to invite God into our lives and maintain a relationship with Him through prayer. Faith believes in all things through prayer and thanksgiving. It is impossible to pray too much. We can pray for protection, forgiveness, guidance, understanding, healing and peace. We can express our love, our gratitude, our needs, our worries, and our fears. We ought to pray boldly and be generous with our prayers for others, especially our leader's whether we like them or not, God has allowed them to be in their position. Trust that God will hear your prayers and respond. Be aware and seek ways that God may be speaking to you. It may not be in the form or timeframe that you are expecting. Faith remembers to always give thanks and praise, throughout the waiting.

Faith encourages us to place God in the center of our lives. Through faith we know God will provide all our needs. We don't get caught up in the material things and allow activities of this world to distract us from living a life that honors God.

Faith believes in abundance even in times there appears to be lack. In the Bible, there is a story about five loaves of bread and two fish. Jesus was able to feed five thousand people with five loaves and two fish because as He broke off each piece of bread, the supply miraculously continued to restore. It was in the breaking that the increase came.

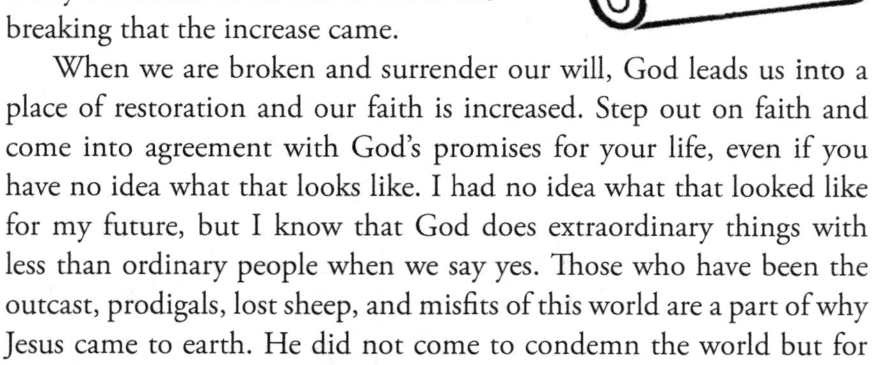

When we are broken and surrender our will, God leads us into a place of restoration and our faith is increased. Step out on faith and come into agreement with God's promises for your life, even if you have no idea what that looks like. I had no idea what that looked like for my future, but I know that God does extraordinary things with less than ordinary people when we say yes. Those who have been the outcast, prodigals, lost sheep, and misfits of this world are a part of why Jesus came to earth. He did not come to condemn the world but for the world to be saved through Him.

Look at Paul. He was a murderer of Christians, but God chose to redeem him and then use him to preach the Good News, the Gospel of Christ. God performed unthinkable great works through him that were radical. God transformed Saul's way of seeing things literally, and in an instant, he stepped into his calling as Paul! Paul wrote at least thirteen letters that are included in the New Testament. God does not call the qualified, He qualifies whom He calls.

As Saul neared Damascus on his journey, suddenly a light from heaven flashed around him and he fell to the ground. He had an encounter with Jesus. The men traveling with Saul stood there speechless; they heard the sound but did not see anyone.

At this moment, his faith in what he could not see strengthened. Paul got up from the ground, but when he opened his eyes, he could see nothing. So, he was led by the hand into Damascus. I encourage you to read more about this story in the book of Acts Chapter 9.

Saul began transforming into Paul! He was forgiven of much and was determined to live a life in radical faith. Think about the previous times in your life God has suddenly done what only He can do. He will do it again!

Stories like these are all throughout the bible. Jesus did not come to help those who had it all together; the church is a hospital for the broken. He came to save the sick in mind, body, and soul.

> John 16:33 NIV- *"I have told you these things so that in me you may have peace. In this world you will have trouble. But take heart! I have overcome the world."*

Faith Carries You Through the Hard Times of Life

Radical faith in Christ means we have peace no matter our circumstances, believing that He already has it worked out in our best interest no matter what it looks like at the moment.

Faith doesn't make anyone exempt from going through tough times or experiencing circumstances that don't make any sense to human understanding. But one thing I do understand is that we are at war in a spiritual battle. Choose to have faith and trust in God with your life and future, no matter what you're going through, He has good things planned for your life.

Have faith that during the wait; heavenly angels are battling with angels of darkness on your behalf. Jesus pleads on our behalf in heaven, and part of this is the ongoing effects of His own death. He covers all sin past, present, and future. Though the battle is already won, we are living it out until Jesus returns. He came as a son of a man riding a mule, but the bible tells us He will appear on a White War Horse when He returns!

Revelation 19:11-16 NKJV-

11 Now I saw heaven opened, and behold, a white horse. And He who sat on him was called Faithful and True, and in righteousness He judges and makes war.

12 His eyes were like a flame of fire, and on His head were many crowns. He had a name written that no one knew except Himself.

13 He was clothed with a robe dipped in blood, and His name is called The Word of God.

14 And the armies in heaven, clothed in fine linen, white and clean, followed Him on white horses.

15 Now out of His mouth goes a sharp sword, that with it He should strike the nations. And He Himself will rule them with a rod of iron. He Himself treads the winepress of the fierceness and wrath of Almighty God.

16 And He has on His robe and on His thigh a name written:

KING OF KINGS AND
LORD OF LORDS.

Faith is looking past the things of this world and pressing onward to the goal of eternity. God created us to do great and mighty things in His name. We allow Him to transform us from the inside out because of our faith and obedience to His voice. Ask Him to speak to you by way of the Holy Spirit. We are not alive just to survive; it is His will for us to love Him, and others well, and thrive.

Being like Christ is your goal, but your journey will last a lifetime. Our journey involves stretching and strengthening our faith through our prayers and worship. We belong to His family and are a part of His body. We also are strengthened through fellowship with other brothers and sisters in Christ. We become who He created us to be through discipleship.

Every living thing starts small. Look how small we are when we are born. As a newborn baby, I didn't have hair on my head until I was two! Yes, I was a little bald baby. My mom used to put a bow on top of my head so that people knew I was a girl. Just think, though, that every small living thing can grow to its full potential when given space, love, and opportunity.

Our Faith in God places all circumstances into His hands while giving us the strength to keep our eyes on divine opportunities and not our situations.

Philippians 4:13 NKJV- *"I can do all things through Christ who strengthens me."*

Stand on this promise- you will do all things through the strength of Christ. Speak these declarations over yourself, your life, your situations, and believe it. Partner with God and receive the power of Christ's spirit that is alive in you and receive it by faith. Write out your visions, don't ever stop dreaming, and have fun doing creative things that excite you.

God will give you the desires of your heart; He is the one who put them there in the first place. Create a vision board using pictures that represent your goals and dreams. Our eyes are the windows to the soul and what you look at, is what you become. If your thoughts don't align with your vision, dismiss them, and step out in faith on what God says about you.

When I agree with the truth about who He says I am, it helps me hear His voice and strengthens my faith. I wasn't sure how to start this book until I listened to that small voice say, "Be still and know that I am God. Just pick up a pen."

So, I did!

We are covered by the blood of Christ, powered by the Holy Spirit, and guided by the Word of God. It wasn't until I started walking in the lead of the Holy Spirit, with God guiding me, that I realized there is so much I've missed out on experiencing. But I have faith that God will restore *all* that the devil has stolen from me, and God will restore all for you too!

Nothing could ever compare to the joy we have when we are walking in freedom through the power of God's love in our life — it's unexplainable. He will take all things and turn them around in your favor. If you haven't already, I encourage you to read about the life of Joseph in the book of Genesis.

The promise over Joseph's life from Genesis 50:20 NIV- is ours for today

> *"You planned to harm me. But God planned it for good. He planned to do what is now being done. The saving of many lives".*

God will use what was intended to destroy you and turn it around in your favor and He will get the Glory for it by anointing you to evangelize and pray for others!

> Romans 8:28 NIV– *"And we know that in all things God works for the good of those who love him, who have been called according to his purpose"*

There was a time I struggled with depression, the root of shame and unforgiveness toward myself opened the door for this manifestation. Sometimes the hardest person to forgive is ourselves.

I didn't want to come out of the house. I didn't want anyone to even look at me. I was uncomfortable in my skin. In my life before Christ, I sought approval from others, entertained demons, used drugs, carelessly spent money, and walked around with a chip on my shoulder. I hid behind false confidence masked as pride. I used material things as a cover-up to hide how lost I was.

I was dressing up the outside to cover up the pain within my soul. I agreed with the lies and deception that I allowed to consume my life. Lies, deception, and distraction are some of the tools in the enemy's tackle box that he will use to keep us in darkness when we lose faith. We allow familiar and accusing spirits to enter by agreeing with lies the devil wants us to believe, which robs us of our faith.

God's Word

God has called me out of the grave- I know He is real, and now, through faith, I believe in who I am as a child of God. We receive a more profound revelation of our Kingdom Identity by studying His Word and having faith in the unseen no matter what is happening around us. So have faith in Him as He opens your eyes to who He created you to be. I promise you it is worth it.

The **BIBLE** is our guide for living life to the fullest:

Basic
Instruction
Before
Leaving
Earth

There are many ways God speaks to His children. Through scriptures, other people, dreams, and visions just to name a few. The bible is alive; God guides us and talks to us in many ways through the Logos- the written word of God and the Rhema word, in the spirit. The Rhema word often occurs while you're reading a particular passage of Scripture. The Logos comes alive, and it may be a scripture you've read many times before. But, depending on what is happening in your life at a particular time or season, you now view it differently and see how it applies to your life personally. God is always speaking to us; He wants us to pay attention, so we hear Him.

When we trust what we cannot see but believe in something greater than our own abilities, it strengthens our faith and ignites our spirit. It often takes the deep despairs and difficulties of life to remind us that part of the ascended role of Jesus Christ is to help the members of His Church through the Holy Spirit. Through the power of the Holy Spirit, we find comfort.

When we trust what we cannot see but believe in something greater than our own abilities, it strengthens our faith and ignites our spirit.

In the Old Testament before Christ, we were governed by the law of Moses. Animals were slaughtered to atone for our sins. But Jesus is the ultimate sacrifice who fulfilled the law.

> Matthew 5:17 ESV- *"Do not think that I have come to abolish the Law or the Prophets; I have not come to abolish them but to fulfill them.*

When Christ fulfilled the law, He earned us the privilege of life. Those who are in Christ, likewise, share in His righteousness and are declared righteous through Him. In that sense, the law has always stood and will continue to stand fulfilled by grace. Jesus is now sitting at the right hand of God interceding on our behalf and has made the power of the Holy Spirit available to us as our ultimate guide and comfort. When the law was introduced, it was never intended to be the instrument by which man would save himself, but it was the instrument through which man was to be saved. Our faith in Christ is our saving grace.

> Psalm 23:4 says ESV- *"Even though I walk through the valley of the shadow of death I will fear no evil for your rod and your staff they comfort me."*

When we allow faith to be our loudest voice, we surrender to God, believing His will is best for us, by allowing Him to guide our lives. God becomes our rod and staff by guiding us through the Holy Spirit.

I know God will always lead us to the best grazing grounds to feed our soul. The word of God waters our seeds of faith so that they will produce good fruit in our lives when nurtured in good soil. We are responsible for the quality of our soil. This begins by loving God, selflessly loving ourselves, and those around us.

You Are No Longer a Slave to Fear

I became conditioned to walking in fear and believed the lies the enemy told me about myself. We can often live in fear and anxiety when we don't know our identity in Christ. Jesus said that the devil is a liar—that he is the father of lies. The devil cannot "make" us do anything, but he is a master deceiver. His job is to deceive people into believing anything that interferes with God's plan. Jesus Christ, in contrast, is called "The Way, The Truth, and the Life," and His plan is for each person to experience life "*more abundantly and to the fullest.*" Through faith in Christ, we believe in God's goodness.

Do not be deceived, the devil uses part truths, twisted with lies that cause us to allow fear to take over. That is where the devil wants us because fear paralyzes us and robs us from living in faith.

Biblical truth sets people free from those fears if they will believe and trust God's Word. One of the biggest deceptions is that God cannot transform you, you're beyond saving, and faith seems far away. When we say I can't, we agree with the lie that stops us before we start. Do not receive that, do not believe that!

God has called you for greatness one step at a time. No matter where you've been or what you've done, your past is not your future, and it doesn't define you. I challenge you to step out in faith and rise above your circumstances. You are an overcomer! Any difficulties or mess you've made in the past is a message that will help set someone else free! Let your faith be the loudest voice you listen to!

If you have asked Jesus to be your Savior, you have been reborn. No matter what anyone says about you, God sees you. I've gone from a dead woman walking and living in the bondage of sin to being renewed through God's word because of His love, mercy, and grace. Jesus took every sin and every curse to that cross when He became sin to save us. When He died on the cross, we were set free, and His blood covered our sins. When He died, He died as us, and when He rose, we rose with Him resurrected from our past!

We have been redeemed and given the same authority as Jesus because He now lives in us. So, for all who have accepted Christ as their Savior, God's promises are yes and amen. This also means our lives are guided by faith in Him and that we don't try to do things independently.

We should depend on what He says about us, His plans for us, and having faith in what He is doing no matter what any circumstances appear to be. The bible tells us that Jesus shows up in your life all the time, is around you all the time, and His spirit is always with us. He shows up in what other people say to you, in opportunities, and she shows up in our problems and difficulties even when we don't pay attention. Throughout the bible, Jesus teaches His disciples about faith. I believe He was showing them how to increase their faith no matter what was going on around them or what people believed to be true because of what the circumstances looked like. In many instances recorded Jesus healed the sick, cleansed lepers, and even raised the dead. I am sure there are many other miracles that were not recorded. He showed up when people least expected it and many times at the last minute. People saw the works of Jesus and began to see themselves and their families healed because of His love and the power of God within Him, and their faith was increased.

Our faith is tested and stretched through the storms of life, which causes us to surrender our control over to something greater than what we as humans could do on our own. God is always in control even when we allow the enemy to add poisonous ingredients to our lives with his lies and schemes. When we get sidetracked, God will use it as an opportunity to increase our faith in who He is, and if we allow it, He will put us right back in position as if we never got sidetracked in the first place.

God always has full authority of what He allows the enemy to do in situations. Our free will allows us to go off-course, but He will never let us handle more than we can bear on our own. However, we must have faith in His will for our lives and trust Him. When we step outside of the will and protection of God in our lives, it is a recipe for disaster that often leads to mental, emotional, and sometimes physical harm. It also opens the doors of anxiety and fear to enter.

I pray that you have increased discernment and walk in authority knowing your Kingdom Identity. Because of who Christ is, we have the authority to overcome the enemy. Sometimes God allows us to face difficult trials that teach us and make us stronger, and through it all we learn to rely on Him, no matter what we face.

> Luke 10:19 NKJV- *"Behold, I give you the authority to trample on serpents and scorpions, and over all the power of the enemy, and nothing shall by any means hurt you."*

God is The Creator of Potential—and The Completer of Fulfillment

We may not yet know that our God given potential exists. When we believe that God has given us every ability to maximize our potential, we believe in faith that we can do all things through Christ who gives us strength. In Christ we have been given authority over fear, anger, frustration, anxiety, depression etc. These are some of the enemy's agents on assignment to enslave us and steal our faith and rob our potential. We must not allow the voice of these agents to speak into our belief system. Knowing our Kingdom Identity gives us power to overcome their schemes. These agents have no power unless you allow it by agreeing with them. Take back the authority you have as a child of

God. You have a choice, keep your eyes on Jesus, walk in faith and He will give you everything you need in this life. Do not allow the devil to attach you to his puppet strings by giving up on your dreams but allow your confidence in Christ to believe in all of your potential. With God all things are possible.

Storms can come to stretch our faith. When you find yourself in the storms of life, keep your eyes above the clouds and remember this too shall pass. The devil likes to torment us to see if we will buckle and bow to him. In Christ you have authority over the devil's schemes, so use it and command the enemy! "Get behind me satan!" The battle has already been won on the cross.

You are a child of God, a son or daughter of the King of Kings. Life is not a fairy tale and having a Hallmark channel life is unrealistic; but having the faith and believing in God will give you the strength to endure while you keep your eyes on Him through all situations. When your life is rooted in faith, you will have peace through life's challenging storms. Through life's tough seasons, faith in God will make you strong. Trust that God's plans are for you to prosper and let that give you hope. Trials are not from God, but sometimes He allows them to teach us, give us a thicker skin and make us stronger. Remember that it is through the process of breaking that our faith is increased. He takes our brokenness and makes us whole.

It is all about perception; the devil wants you to see yourself as defeated. Remember who God says you are. You can do all things through Christ who gives you strength. God understands everything we feel and go through. He walked the earth, as a human man with feelings and emotions. He has felt what we go through and sympathizes with our weaknesses.

The Fruit of the Holy Spirit is a biblical term that sums up the nine attributes of a person or community living in accord with the Holy Spirit, according to Galatians 5:22-23 ESV- "*But the fruit of the Spirit is love, joy, peace, patience, kindness, goodness, faithfulness, gentleness, self-control; against such things there is no law.*"

Some versions translate that our self-control is long-suffering. God doesn't want us to suffer, but He wants us to have faith in Him as our comforter in times of long waiting or suffering. When we focus on Him and His promises, life's trials will not shake us. Our faith journey began when we believed that by His blood we are saved and by His stripes we are healed.

We secure our freedom with consistency. When I get up in the morning, I start my day in prayer, agreeing with God's promises over my life. The trajectory of my day is set by what comes out of my mouth. This is what I call an atmosphere shifting prayer.

I begin by thanking God for filling my lungs with His breath. Thank you, Father, for the air I breathe. Thank you, Father, for waking me up today. Thank you, Father, for my salvation and your protection over me. Thank you for loving and guiding me. Thank you for allowing me to be your servant. Show me what You have for me today. How can I please you today, Lord?

Whatever you want to say to God—say it! He loves it when you seek Him. I have conversations with God all day, every day. I walk around talking to Him all the time. My talks with Him are like having a conversation with my best friend. He is my Father, and friend – my best friend – and He wants to be yours too. They say it takes thirty days to develop a new habit. So, for the next thirty days, I challenge you to open your eyes each morning and before your feet hit the floor, open your mouth, and fill your atmosphere with thanks and praise. God will partner with your faith because of who He is and how much He loves you.

When you are excited and want to pick up your phone to share and talk over something with a friend, stop and talk it over with God. Is it His will, our will, or a distraction from the devil to throw us off course? If anyone told me to do this before I was walking in my identity as a child of God, I would say they were crazy, but I can assure you I am the sanest I have ever been. Especially in times of trial, talks with the Father keep us postured in a perfect position to increase our faith in Him.

Psalms 91:1-16 NIV-

Whoever dwells in the shelter of the Most High will rest in the shadow of the Almighty. I will say of the Lord, "He is my refuge and my fortress, my God, in whom I trust." Surely he will save you from the fowler's snare and from the deadly pestilence. He will cover you with his feathers, and under his wings you will find refuge; his faithfulness will be your shield and rampart. You will not fear the terror of night, nor the arrow that flies by day, nor the pestilence that stalks in the darkness, nor the plague that destroys at midday. A thousand may fall at your side, ten thousand at your right hand, but it will not come near you. You will only observe with your eyes and see the punishment of the wicked. If you say, "The Lord is my refuge," and you make the Most High your dwelling, no harm will overtake you, no disaster will come near your tent.

For he will command his angels concerning you to guard you in all your ways; they will lift you up in their hands, so that you will not strike your foot against a stone. You will tread on the lion and the cobra; you will trample the great lion and the serpent. "Because he loves me," says the Lord, "I will rescue him; I will protect him, for he acknowledges my name. He will call on me, and I will answer him; I will be with him in trouble, I will deliver him and honor him. With long life I will satisfy him and show him my salvation."

The Bible doesn't say problems won't come; scriptures give us comfort during hard times and encourage us to believe that God is with us in times of trouble.

Faith comes from within the eyes of your heart. Believers see things as God intended by being in a relationship with Him. The reality is that life is not going to be an easy road, but I can promise you this, one day with Christ is better than a thousand days without Him. Faith believes that you are living, breathing, and walking in His light from the core of your soul. It comes with a promise that He will never leave or abandon us no matter what the world says.

Hebrews 11:1 KJV- *"Now faith is the substance of things hoped for, the evidence of things not seen."*

There is faith and then there is hope. Hope is when you want something to happen, it may be something you'd like to have or do. They are distinct yet different. Faith is complete trust or confidence in someone or something.

Faith is confidence in what we hope for, yet what happens to our faith when what we hoped for does not happen? Do you give up or do you believe in the promises of God, trusting by faith that ultimately, everything is working out for the good of His plan and purpose for your life?

My testimony is very broad, but I'd like to share with you a time God told me to trust Him in faith and what He will do when we actively trust His plans for our lives no matter what.

In 2011 I had just moved to California. I was working for a company that did not model or conduct their services in good business ethics. They were under investigation by the FBI for charges of fraud. While employed by this company upon arrival each morning for work, I sensed an unsettling in my spirit. The probation department and pre-trial investigators were strolling through the office, interviewing, and investigating the owners. My criminal history made me extremely uncomfortable as I'm sure it would anyone, even if they didn't have a past involving a crime.

One day while alone at my house in prayer, a news broadcast channel was on my television. I was outside on my patio speaking to the Lord God, "I can't continue to work for these people and I'm very uncomfortable. What do you have for me, Lord? What do You want me to do?"

Just as I asked these questions, the news broadcaster said, "social media is taking over the industry by storm". A lightbulb went on in my head and I heard the voice of God. Believing in His promises, I stepped out in faith by opening an online marketing firm for social media. I had no idea what I was doing but I trusted in blind faith what I knew God was telling me to do.

There were many, many obstacles, I won't get into the details, but by faith I believed what I heard God tell me. In February 2022 eleven years later, my business had grown into a full-blown online marketing firm. Funny thing is that I am not tech savvy at all. I can send a text message and email but anything much more than that I'm not well-versed in.

Everything is by faith, asking the Holy Spirit to guide me, and believing I can do all things through Christ! God is capable of *all* things, and He likes to show off through us by doing something that *blows our minds.* All I can say is, it's all God working through me because of my faith in Him! He wants to show off through you too! Will you answer the call?

When things don't go as we would like them to, I believe that God has a different plan for us. It may not necessarily look like what we had hoped for, but I do know God's plans are much better than what we could imagine. I do not know what is best for me. Anytime I've tried to do things without God's guidance, I messed it up. This is truly where a test of our faith comes in. Faith is knowing without a doubt that His ways are higher than my ways and His thoughts are higher than my thoughts. Walking in faith means believing that He knows exactly what is best for me and I trust Him fully.

God is looking for those who are willing and obedient. He wants to bless us. His eyes are searching the earth to show Himself mighty and strong in us. Look at Abraham, who became known as the "father of faith."

God tested his faith, commanding that he kill his only heir. Trusting Him, Abraham almost carried out this act before God stopped him. To reward his faith, God promised that he would be the father of many nations. He became the forefather of all generations.

God wants to speak to you, open your spiritual ear by faith, seek His guidance, and respond in obedience to what He says to you. Believing in something greater than ourselves will transform our way of thinking into a faithful mindset. Faith is like a spiritual seed that plants thoughts in our minds that shift our mental patterns. Just have faith of a mustard seed. Trust the

process. Have faith that it will grow, nurture and care for that seed. That seed, my dear friend, is you!

This is what happens when we put our faith in something we do not see. God takes over and nurtures us to where we are supposed to be, no matter what we may have hoped for. Our faith carries us through knowing He is working it all out even when we do not see it. When we are pushing through trials while standing on faith, our roots grow deeper. The deeper the roots, the stronger our faith.

Living in faith means knowing that when we trust Him, we are moving to where He wants us to be. He wants good things for us. When we take back our will and let the desires of our flesh take over, we are letting go of faith. This is when the devil digs into his box of lies and deception. Guard your hearts and minds in Christ Jesus. Always. We have authority to stomp out lies and crush the enemy's head before they start playing tricks on our minds. Our battlefield begins in our minds. Do you know God? The evidence of our faith is not in something we see, it's in someone we know!

The world tells us to believe in things we don't see all the time through TV and even through movies.

Do you remember the Wizard of Oz? Dorothy got taken away by a tornado to the land far, far away called Oz. The people of Oz instructed her to follow the yellow brick road by faith. Along the way she brought hope to the lost. It's kind of ironic because even though she was lost trying to find her way home, she encouraged those along the way—helping the Lion, Tin Man and the Scarecrow find their gifts, which eventually led to her finding her own. Of course, she had the wicked witch on her tail at every turn trying to deceive her, but she put faith in something she could not see—Oz, the man behind the curtain. She listened to her heart, stepped out in faith, and followed the yellow brick road.

This is how some of us may feel our lives have been. Thrown off course by disappointments, family dysfunction, hurts, broken marriages- our life's tornado took us to a land far, far away. Yet the unseen man, God, who is in control is lining things up for us while we are not even aware of what life has in store. The best is yet to come when we stand on His promises, and I am a living witness of a loving God.

No one can ever tell me different! His promises are true. He has shown me repeatedly through all my failures, setbacks, and disappointments that He was there protecting me along the way. In the Wizard of Oz, Dorothy was sent out to speak life into those around her, all while she was trying to find her way home. This is what God calls us to do, feed His sheep meaning we are to love the broken, bring hope to the hopeless and pray for the sick and the lost.

The living God creator of all the universe knows us and cares about us. He sees us from somewhere beyond the clouds, though He is unseen, yet He is always there. He waits for us to realize who we are in Him. He wants us to believe in our Kingdom Identity and let faith be the loudest voice.

In Christ Jesus, our disappointments turn into divine appointments that are all a part of His love story for our life. He loves each of us uniquely! So much so that He designed each of us with a unique fingerprint, eye retina and DNA.

Yet, we are all made in His image. His design of nature, the earth, the ocean, the living creatures, the universe, the stars.

Step out in faith and give God permission to guide you by trusting in Him, especially through the storms.

Chapter 3

Unveiling of the Heart

Today, the media influences our minds and hearts more than ever. We must guard our gates, which are our eyes and ears that can affect our thoughts and feelings. The news, television shows, social media all supply the public with an information overload. Some true, some false, some negative, some positive, but it all contributes to shaping the thinking process.

We cannot control the information released by the media, but we can manage what we participate in, how we process different circumstances, and what we hold onto in our minds and hearts. Therefore, we need to be protective of the influences we open ourselves up to. Many of the things we feed our minds and hearts with do not align with God's plans for our lives. You cannot become what God has planned for you to become in life until you understand what influences your identity. We are all subject to things that happen to us and around us in our environment. It is vital to be mindful of what you listen to, and the company you keep. Toxic company corrupts the mind and hurts our hearts.

> 1 Corinthians 15:33 ESV- *"Do not be deceived: "Bad company ruins good morals."*

We have free will and control over what we choose to participate in. Evil companions will corrupt good morals and character.

We cannot restrict the flow of information that bombards us, but we can ask God to help us each day to stay focused on Him and to shape our thoughts by being in His presence. Seeking guidance through the power of the Holy Spirit in our lives will strengthen us, and our desire to do what is right grows stronger. When our hearts are surrendered, our prayers are like hot coals placed on the altar of fire before God. What incredible hope God offers us, to be able to have a new, changed heart. When we put off our old expectations, and regulations of religion, we put on our new self in Christ through a relationship with our Savior.

Do not allow the world around you to fit you into its mold; instead, be diligent in your quest to renew your mind and soften your heart. The Bible is a guidebook with instructions on staying in tune with God's purpose for our lives. More times than not, God will give us only a part of what He wants us to do at one time; it is like being handed pieces of a puzzle. If He gave us more than that, we may become overwhelmed and wouldn't be able to handle it.

Allow God to transform you into a new person by changing how you think, and He too will soften your heart. When you consistently feed yourself with God's Word, you will be guided on the right path to reach your destiny.

When we are walking in brokenness, we attract brokenness and see others and the world around us from a wounded and hardened heart. Maybe because of the house we were raised in and the things we were exposed to, maybe our perception of normal has become distorted. Sometimes what we view as healthy is *broken* because it's all we have known.

But what if we don't know who we are? When the eyes of our hearts are closed, we believe that keeping people at a distance keeps us safe from rejection and shelters us from shame, judgment, and hurt.

When the eyes of our heart have been opened, we see ourselves and others the way the Father sees us. When God looks at us, He looks through the lens of what Jesus did at the cross and His love for us. Our hearts are softened, and we begin to believe in His love for us; we take ownership of the truth that we are His children and worthy of all the good things He has for us in this life. He is a King, and as His children, that makes us royalty.

God has many great gifts He wants to give to us in this lifetime and for eternity. God gives each of us gifts and talents, but we are responsible to develop three areas of our life for our gifts to be fully unlocked and used by God. Our spiritual connection with God, our character, and our hearts. As His children, we have an inheritance in Heaven that God is keeping for all His people. God has reserved for Himself a portion of all the peoples of the earth to be His special possession, His treasured possession, His chosen people, and has made available to us the Fruits of the Spirit. Love, joy, peace, patience, kindness, goodness, faithfulness, gentleness, and self-control.

Before the eyes of my heart were opened, I saw things from a worldly perspective. I looked for acceptance in counterfeit people I thought were my friends and a false sense of comfort in money and things. My heart was blind, and I believed happiness was found in material things, prestige, and status. My worldly view was that if I had a nice car, stylish clothes, status, and money, that my heart would be full, and everything would be great right? Well, that is the farthest thing from the truth.

Because of life's experiences, the eyes of my heart were shut, and my lenses were blurred to who I was and how God saw me.

Do not allow the world's demands to shape your heart into what God doesn't want you to become or who He hasn't called you to be. Our Kingdom Identity separates us from the world and gives us a new perspective on the enemy's tactics and how we see things.

God wants the eyes of our hearts to be open and enlightened so that we walk in truth, and it begins with the healing of the heart, freedom from oppression, and a personal encounter with God. The good news of the Gospel is that Jesus is passionate about healing the whole person, and He has invited us to come alongside Him in this mission.

Guard your heart and mind in Christ Jesus.

Apply your heart, eyes, and ears to words of knowledge and follow His instructions. The heart in scripture signifies the seat of affection, wisdom, and understanding. The heart is a seat of our emotions that we must learn to master in Christ.

It is the Lord Himself, who calls upon us asking My son or daughter, come to me all who are weary, and I will give you rest. What He is asking for is our heart. He wants us to be in an intimate relationship with Him: He calls us My son or My daughter, we have been born to this world through our parents, but He is our Creator. He addresses men and women everywhere, for He is the Father of all mankind in this sense.

Acts 17:28 NIV- *"For in Him we live and move and have our being. As some of your own poets have said, 'We are his offspring'."*

God made humanity. But there is a more profound and intimate sense in which we need to become the children of God. The Unveiling of our heart comes from believing the truth about how He sees us, and by walking in faith.

Galatians 3:26 NIV- *"So in Christ Jesus, you are all children of God through faith."*

The triune God is 3 in One. God wrapped Himself in the flesh and came to earth as a man, Jesus. When Jesus ascended into Heaven, He sent the gift of the Holy Spirit to guide and comfort us. Christ comes to live in our hearts when we accept Him as our Lord and Savior. God's love has been poured into our hearts through the Holy Spirit. When we surrender our lives to Him, then our hearts begin to change. God can transform us when we believe He has plans to prosper us and to give us hope and a future.

God requests that we invite Him in and allow Him to love us. My son or daughter, give me your heart. God is inviting us in and calling us His children. He is asking us to give Him our heart, which really means all of ourselves, our selfish desires, our whole being. The fact that God seeks us out and then asks for our hearts proves His great love for us. We now learn to love because *He first loved us*. This is also a requirement on our part. When Jesus says to us, "Give me your heart."

He wants all of us.

Exchange of the Heart

When we give God our hearts, He then exchanges them from bitter to sweet, from selfish to serving.

We see a promise from the Lord, In Ezekiel 36:26 NKJV- "*I will give you a new heart and put a new spirit within you; I will take the heart of stone out of your flesh and give you a heart of flesh.*"

This is the message of the Gospel, and if we ask why we need a new heart, the Bible tells us that our heart is unclean and that it is hard and therefore cold. In exchange, God offers us a heart that is clean, pure, tender, and warm. He does not offer to patch up the old heart. Instead, He invites us to be made new through our Identity in His Kingdom.

> 2 Corinthians 5:17 NKJV- "*Therefore, if anyone is in Christ, he is a new creation; old things have passed away; behold, all things have become new.*"

If you have not done so, will you give Him your old heart and let Him give you His new one?"

He loves us with an everlasting love, and until you've experienced the Love of the Heavenly Father, I believe you've not truly lived! In replacing our old hearts, we die inside to our bitterness, selfishness, and wickedness. He replaces it with forgiveness, selflessness, and kindness.

If you've accepted Jesus as your Savior, you have then been resurrected with Christ and through learning about Him you begin to walk in His Love. Jesus not only died *for you*, but He also died *as you*! He took on your sin, and when He rose, you rose with Him!

When we see the heart of God, we then see ourselves as He sees us. This is Kingdom Identity. Religion makes us prove worthiness, and we run from it because not one of us is without sin. But the Love of God through our Kingdom Identity makes us want to stay!

Our Hearts are what God uses to Establish Us in His Kingdom.

> In Ezekiel 36:28 NIV- God says, "*Then you will live in the land I gave to your ancestors, you will be my people, and I will be your God*"

The primary reference in these words is to Israel's restoration. For years the Jews were scattered throughout the earth, but the Bible promises in the end, they will all go back to their own land to live there. All of this is a parable for us to return to our first love, God. Our hearts have wandered over the earth, and there has been nowhere to rest; but God says, "*Give me your heart,* and I will cause it to live in the land; I will establish it."

The trouble with our hearts is that it wanders; it cannot rest without the spirit of truth indwelling within our hearts.

King David knew what it was to have a steadfast and established heart.

Psalm 57:7 NIV- *"My heart, O God, is steadfast, my heart is steadfast; I will sing and make music."*

With so many distractions all around us, singing praise to God from our heart strengthens our faith and carries a healing anointing. Open your mouth and praise God for who He is, especially in these days of crisis, turmoil, and fear! Praise and worship grounds us; it releases angelic activity to partner with our praise and throws the devil off course. I've seen people healed during worship without anyone laying a hand on them or praying for them! Healed by praising and worshiping God.

We have a steadfast heart because we are united with The One true living God who is always doing a new thing yet, He never changes. He wants our hearts to be established in Him. God knew you before the beginning of time, and He loves you! But there is another reason why we need to have our hearts established, *once we are established He can empower us*!

God desires to empower us. He wants our hearts surrendered to Him so He can empower us with His Spirit and prepare us for His Love to be released through us, and into the world around us.

In Ezekiel 36:27 NIV- *"I will put my Spirit in you and move you to follow my decrees and be careful to keep my laws."*

God gives us a new way of looking at the world, ourselves, and others. When the eyes of our hearts open, He gives us His power and guides our paths and what ways to walk in. We cannot be moved to follow His decrees on our own, but God will enable us to do this by the indwelling Person (Christ in us) and through the guidance of the Holy Spirit residing on the inside of our hearts.

You were indwelled with a gift of the Holy Spirit the moment you received Christ. This is what Kingdom Identity is all about. We cannot live it through our own hearts, but God says He will come and dwell within us to help us as we walk in ways that please Him. This is another reason why God wants your heart so that He can empower it.

His love enriches us. He also wants our hearts so He can enrich our lives! Have you ever felt like something was missing, but you didn't know what it was?

Without knowing our Kingdom Identity, every person is walking around with a hole in their heart, and if you let God fill you, then you'll be complete in Him no matter what life throws at you. God isn't a quick fix on the road to personal happiness. He is God. He is not content with just a corner of your heart. He is the One who Rules All things. He is the one who provides every good and perfect gift.

He wants your whole heart so your entire life can be enriched. He is a good Father and wants the best for you. When you give your heart to Him, He pours out His goodness and mercy on you.

Philippians 4:19 NIV- *"And my God will meet all your needs according to the riches of His glory in Christ Jesus."*

We have free will and make our own decisions, but He is supreme overall. He will turn All things around for the good of those who love Him and are called according to His purpose.

If you haven't already, will you give Him your heart, so that He may enrich your entire life? Maybe you believe you don't have anything to give God and are possibly ashamed of experiences from your past. But He loves you just as you are, and He needs your whole heart for Him to enrich the rest of your life.

If you give Him your heart, He will *exchange it, empower it, establish it, and enrich it* while restoring and renewing the broken pieces. I'm here as a walking, living, breathing witness. God's timing is always perfect, so don't beat yourself up. I say this because I wished I had done it sooner, but when I gave Him my heart, He began doing things in me that no man or medicine could ever do!

My parents were babies raising a baby, and they had no idea of what Kingdom Identity was. My father was Catholic, but my mom had a fire within her, and she took me to a Pentecostal church when I was 13. People were speaking in tongues and dancing up and down the aisles.

I felt like I finally found what was missing

They asked if anyone wanted to receive Christ, and my hand shot up in the air and I received Christ. That day I got *slain in the spirit* and was laid out on the floor. My mom says I laid down in the middle of the service and went to sleep, but I know different!

I am a natural-born seer, and from a very young age, I would see things and feel things in the spirit. I didn't fit in anywhere and felt like I was an outcast from the start. I had a make-believe friend I would ask to protect me when the darkness tried to overtake me.

My mom told me that those believed to be witches were burned at the stake during the early days in Scotland. I now believe many of them were misunderstood prophets and healers that the devil robbed of their Kingdom Identity. I recently learned that my mom's sister, my Auntie, is a known healer. There are many different spirits, and other than being under the anointing through the power of the Holy Spirit, the rest are extremely dangerous.

No one around me knew anything about the supernatural, and it was looked at as a bad thing. My Father told me that I was seeking attention, so I was frequently sent to my room and spent most of my childhood alone.

My earthly father broke my heart from a very young age. This was when fear moved in to torment me. I would lay on my back in bed at night because I could feel the darkness lie on top of me like a sheet. It would often paralyze me, so I couldn't move, and I couldn't talk. I was struck with fear, frozen in my bed, scared and alone. I would hear what sounded like the footsteps of thousands of armies marching. I now know this was a legion of armies trying to torment me. I didn't know about the armor of God so I would pull the covers over my head, or I would go inside my closet to try and hide.

All these things opened doors for the devil to try and steal my identity at a very young age. Pay attention to your children; they are gifted beyond what we could imagine. Allow the Creator to be creative in their minds and hearts. Pour into future generations by encouraging them and speaking life and love over your children. There is no Junior Holy Spirit; children are gifted! Our future generations depend on you to protect the hearts of the children, the innocent, the broken, and the lost.

Misunderstood and rejected, I began hanging out with a bad crowd. My heart and mind were naive and vulnerable to the wickedness of the world. I always saw the potential in people and the goodness inside them. I saw things for what they could be, yet not facing the reality of what they were. This led me to disappointment, isolation, depression, and an indescribable place of emptiness. I had no idea who I was, and I continually spiraled downward. Unfortunately, that is precisely where the enemy wants us. The spiritual realm is real, and the thief comes only to rob, kill, and destroy.

> Ephesians 6:12 NIV- *"For our struggle is not against flesh and blood, but against the rulers, against the authorities, against the powers of this dark world, and against the spiritual forces of evil in the heavenly realms."*

When God isn't the ruler of our hearts, and we don't know our Kingdom Identity, we wander the earth looking for a place to fit in and where we belong, which inevitably leads to a dead end.

Before I knew how much God loved me, I didn't feel worthy or good enough. I didn't understand that my identity was stripped from me since childhood, I was led astray by the devil and sent out wandering in the wilderness. I didn't realize that the people I was involved with were just as broken as I was. People who are hurt, hurt other people.

My picker was broken. If you were hurting and spiritually crushed, that was a green light for me to fix you and bring out the best in you. But it brought out the worst in both of us in all actuality.

There's an old saying, "People bring you down before you bring them up." I really didn't have an "up" to bring anyone to because I too was broken. I became more broken by taking on the brokenness of others. I cannot fix anyone, I am not God, I always ended up hitting a brick wall.

Another old saying - "You can lead a horse to water, but you can't make them drink". What happens when we ourselves aren't drinking the water? How can we lead anyone anywhere? We all have had experiences that have taken us down a rough road, some of us harder than others.

Some of us get stuck in a revolving door because by doing what we always did, we will get what we always got. It's hard to know what freedom is like if you've been in bondage your whole life. It's crazy how pain is a motivator for change, but it is. Pain seeks pleasure, and this world's satisfaction only leads to brokenness, trouble and destruction. I had to ask God to adjust the lens I was looking through and allow Him to turn it to a different viewpoint. Instead of trying to fix everyone else, I needed to focus on myself.

I had to come to terms with the fact that it's not my job to fix anyone else. The reality is that by looking outside of ourselves into everyone else's problems, it's a way for us to avoid what a mess our backyard is and how broken our own hearts really are.

Thinking we can fix other people is a recipe for disaster. It will never work like that. What happens is, when people don't respond to your helping them and you want them to be healed more than they want it for themselves, internally, anxiety and anger begin to control you. We can't change or fix people; you can't control or fix others no matter how much potential you see in someone. What is impossible with man is possible with God. It's our job at times to plant seeds, and other times it may be our job to water them, yet only God makes things grow.

When we give our loyalty to the wrong people, we become bound to expectations that go unfulfilled. The only one who will never let us down is God. Even when hard times of life come, when faith is the voice we listen to, we realize that He will turn things around for our good. An enriched heart stays in expectation of good things, and we view trials as an opportunity to make us better and not bitter.

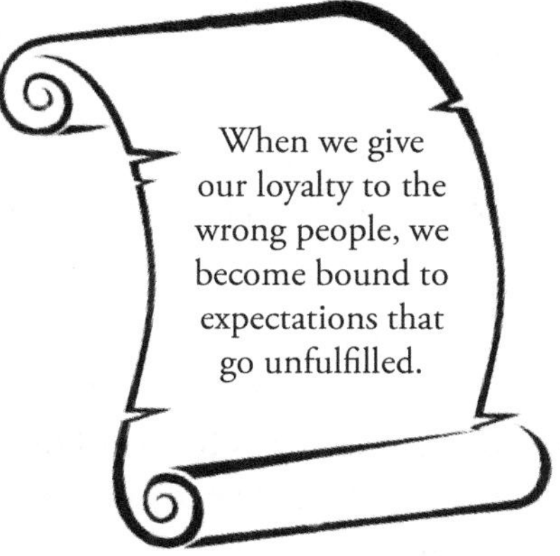

We have all been assigned a measure of faith, and all we need is faith the size of a mustard seed. Even if you don't know where to start, give your heart to God, and everything else will fall in place. Thank you for sharing this journey with me and allowing me to share some of my story and the heart of God with you.

We learn to love ourselves and love others only through encountering God's love first. We need to speak life into people and tell them how God sees them. The future begins with you; souls assigned to you are waiting for you to find them and tell them about the Love of God. Not to fix them, that's God's job!

I was looking to fix others as a coping mechanism to avoid looking at who I was and what I needed to let go of. I needed to forgive those who had hurt me and be healed. Usually, when we focus on someone else, we avoid looking at ourselves. You aren't responsible for the things other people may have done to you or even things you have been through that you thought would work out differently. Maybe you've made some bad choices. What we are responsible for is our own healing and freedom. The only way I have ever found freedom is by surrendering my life wholeheartedly to Christ and by seeking the guidance and comfort of the Holy Spirit.

When we choose to be involved with someone just as messed up as we are, it's a distraction from our own pain. You are attracted to who you are. If you are broken, your attraction is another broken person. If you're happy, joyous, and free, you will attract happy, joyous, and free people. Personal integrity is where we grow in spiritual prosperity.

Your past does not define you!

When we allow God to begin a work in us through the transformation of our hearts, we begin to experience the restoration that only God can bring. He puts His Word of life inside of us. When we are transforming from the inside out, we begin to see things differently. I'm not saying to overlook the lost and hurting; I am saying to love broken people and speak hope and life into them. The rest is God's job, not mine or yours. It is our job to be the best we can be for ourselves, and then we will be prepared for what God originally designed us for in the first place, which is to love Him first above all. Every good and perfect gift comes from God. It begins with a heart that is confident of who we are in Him. Once this transformation takes place, you will find freedom and peace in all you do. Transformation begins even while we are in brokenness. When we are transformed, we begin to see differently and start to attract new things.

Keep in mind you can't plant one good seed and expect to receive a fruitful harvest. It's a constant process of tearing down, pulling out past roots, planting new seeds, and breaking into new ground. I recommend tilling the soil from within your soul, so no particles of familiarity can re-root. For me, freedom from soul wounds and heart-renewal happened through inner emotional healing and deliverance sessions and allowed me to see myself how Jesus sees me. There is a pruning that must take place to get rid of things that are harmful to us. A sort of crushing process to remove old thinking patterns, and new seeds are then planted into the good soil of a renewed heart.

> John 15:5 NIV- *"I am the vine; you are the branches. If you remain in me and I in you, you will bear much fruit; apart from me, you can do Nothing."*

Remain in the vine, we are the branches He is the vine.

When we attempt to do things on our own, or in what our flesh wants us to do, we struggle no matter how hard we try. Our flesh wants to feed selfish desires, and in my experience, those were the things that felt good to me at the time but were bad for me. Things that may look good to you aren't necessarily good for you.

Sometimes we may build a wall around our hearts as a structure of self-protection. We may believe this is a legitimate boundary that keeps us safe; however, walls also limit our connection to God and others. God wants to be the protector in our lives, but first, we must let go of bitterness.

Forgiveness is a big one; there's a heart transplant that takes place through forgiveness. Forgiving your abuser or whoever has hurt you does not condone the bad behavior. What it does is free you from carrying around a bitter heart towards them or anyone who may remind you of them.

When someone hurts you, it's your choice to either hold on to anger, resentment, and thoughts of revenge or let go of the poison and toxicity through forgiveness and move forward.

Who hasn't been hurt by the actions or words of another? Perhaps a parent constantly criticized you growing up, a colleague sabotaged a project, or your husband or wife had an affair. These wounds can leave you with feelings of anger and bitterness, maybe even vengeance and revenge.

Having an unforgiving spirit usually begins with resentment. Resentment develops when you hold a grudge and become inwardly bitter. If you don't practice forgiveness, you might be the one who pays dearly. You become preoccupied with hate and self-pity. Unforgiveness can cause several physical burdens.

Resist resentment and revenge. By embracing forgiveness, you can also embrace peace, hope, gratitude, and joy. Consider how forgiveness can lead you down the path of physical, emotional, and spiritual well-being. In addition, forgiveness will give you a sense of freedom. Forgiveness means different things to different people. Generally, however, it involves a decision to let go of resentment and thoughts of revenge.

The act that hurt or offended you might always be with you, but forgiveness can lessen its grip on you and help free you from the control of the person who harmed you. Forgiveness can even lead to feelings of understanding, empathy, and compassion toward the one who hurt you.

By forgiving them, you release yourself from being held in bondage. What I mean by this is when I forgave those who have hurt me, it was then that they no longer held me captive. Forgiveness is not necessarily for them but for our own peace and releases us from hurt, pain, resentment, anger, anxiety, fear, and much more. These forms of bitterness hurt us much more than the offender. Forgiveness allows us to live for now and allows us to heal and feel the love of the Father. It allows us to move forward and release our pain and gives God permission to renew our hearts.

Keep in mind forgiveness and trust are not the same. I was in an emotionally abusive relationship. Yet, there was goodness I saw in this other person but that doesn't mean I needed to trust them once the trust was broken. Maybe it's because I've always seen the best in people, but I hurt myself in the process. Everyone deserves to be treated with love, kindness, and respect.

You are worthy of love. You are chosen and set apart for His great works. No matter where you've been or what you've done. Don't allow it to infect your heart. Your future is full of promises, and your freedom comes through Christ. A transformed heart lives in peace, love, and joy! Christ provides peace through the hard times when we keep God's love in our hearts.

God does not want His beloved children to be abused. Sometimes God allows us to go through things to stretch and grow us into who He wants us to be for His glory. I never thought I would be where I am today, and it's only through God's grace, love, and mercy that He calls me His own. There is Nothing I have done to deserve the love that God gives me every minute of every day. He wants you to have that love as well, and all you need to do is say yes.

It's in our darkest moments when we give our hearts to Him, surrendering all our struggles and pain of past experiences, that He shows up. He wants to love you more than you want to be loved. He created us to love Him first. God wants us to look to Him for guidance throughout life's journey. Sometimes we need to step back out of our situations and look at things from a different perspective. Sometimes we must put relationships with other people on pause so we can draw close and near to Him for Him to redirect our paths.

Our heart needs to be in a place of good cheer. Stress and fear no longer have a place in our lives because we have the spirit of hope, faith, and the Love of Christ in our hearts. Being around people who pour life into you instead of crushing your spirit is crucial to your wellbeing, growth, and spiritual health. Not everyone is for you. Sometimes, people want to be around you because they want to be involved in what you're doing, maybe others are attracted to a title you carry. But you need people around you who care about you for who you are as a child of God. People who see you truly for you and nourish the heart of God that is within you.

We are of a different Kingdom than this world. We live in it, but we are not of this world. Our home is in Heaven for eternity. Come into agreement with the power of the Holy Spirit for your life, purpose, and destiny. Believe in the good things God has for you. Take heart from that belief system, and you will grow into the person God has created and called you to be.

In Christ, we are complete and completely righteous. For we live in Christ, and He lives within us. Not because of anything we have or haven't done to make us righteous in heart, we are all sinners it's because of Jesus and how much God loves us. God's Spirit is alive within us, and because of Jesus, that makes us an authoritative force not to be reckoned with.

God has imparted into us His gifts by the power of the Holy Spirit. When we surrender to Him, He gives us a new heart made of flesh and removes the heart of stone. Change in your heart begins by changing your beliefs. For transformation to take place, our heart needs to be inclined toward God from within. A surrendered heart postures in submission to God by reading His Word and seeking His will for our lives. Setting our hearts and minds on the things above isn't a one-time task. It's a daily one and sometimes needs to be reset, and checked throughout the day, weeks, months, years, and over a lifetime.

Open your heart and allow God to control every area of your life. When we try to maintain control through selfish desires, we lose control and are never happy. In all reality, we never had control in the first place; the one who has all control is God. Don't give up on your dreams and desires but take the pressure off yourself by trusting in God's timing, and don't stop believing in good things for your life even if you don't see them yet. Guard your heart in Christ, for He is the giver of life and brings joy. We need our hearts to be aligned with Him on purpose.

Chapter 4

Trusting God Even When We Do Not See It in The Natural

Proverbs 3:5-6 NIV- *"Trust in the Lord with all your heart and lean not on your own understanding; in all your ways, submit to Him, and He will make your paths straight."*

Trust is a 5-letter word that carries an incredibly significant meaning! It is a choice. When we choose to depend on our own understanding, we act as if we are more intelligent, wiser, and more authoritative than the creator of the universe.

God created you; He loves you and knows you better than you know yourself. We will go through this life not knowing or understanding a lot of things. The fact that God is all-knowing gives Him the ability to see what lies ahead of us. He knows what we need to become the person He created us to be, all we need to do is trust God and do good. God also knows what needs to happen and which direction we need to go in to receive the blessings He wants to give us. We are children of God, and though we are on this earth, we are *Not of This World*; our eternal destiny is Heaven.

It is not a question of, "Will we face trials and struggles?" Instead, the question is: "Who will we turn to and put our trust in during our times of struggles?"

Submit to God, and He will make your paths straight.

The quality of our life depends on how we respond to things that happen to us and around us. Life is not predictable. There are difficulties along the way. Trusting God in good times can seem easy but trusting God through tough times can be challenging. However, God's unchanging character gives us something to trust in when things feel unsteady and uncertain.

How do you trust that God is good in uncertain circumstances? How do you trust God when you do not understand what is happening and do not see a resolution? These are all valid questions, and God wants to help guide you through them. By submitting, we are under the authority of another. When we submit to God, we surrender our lives and will to His authority, power, and control.

The scripture does not say trust in your feelings, thoughts, emotions, will, or people. Instead, it says we are to *trust in the Lord* with all our heart and lean not on our own understanding. Sometimes, people want to be there for you, but they may need the same thing you need and cannot be there for you. As a result, and not necessarily intentionally, people will let you down.

When we trust in His divine direction for our lives, we position ourselves to hear His voice and are obedient by trusting the process. God is an on-time God; we need to have faith and pray through our waiting seasons. Trust is to believe in reliability, truth, ability, or strength. Trusting God, it means believing in His trustworthiness, His Word, His power, His timing, and His strength. The Bible says that God cannot lie. That He always keeps His promises, He loves you and has good in store for you. By trusting in God this means believing what He says about Himself, and you are true and accurate.

Trusting God is a choice, not just a feeling. So how exactly can we trust God in our everyday life? It is believing in something bigger than yourself even when your emotions or circumstances would have you believe something different. Your feelings and circumstances matter; they are important and very much worth paying attention to. God cares about them both. But emotions alone are not reliable enough to base your life's decisions around. Do not make any permanent decisions based on temporary situations or circumstances. Like winter, spring, summer, and fall, we go through different seasons of life. Feelings and circumstances can change at any moment, in the blink of an eye, in an instant. God, on the other hand, does not change. He is the same yesterday, today, and tomorrow; therefore, He is worthy of your trust.

When you trust someone, you are comfortable being honest and open with them about anything. However, God is much more reliable than even your most trustworthy friend. When things are difficult, He does not want you to keep those struggles to yourself. Trusting God is living a life of obedience and believing in His plans even when things are complicated. I'm not suggesting that you ignore your feelings, the reality of your circumstances or that you pretend that everything is ok when it isn't. Life will have its struggles, and we will experience trials, but by trusting God in and through all things, He works it out in His perfect timing. We will have our moments, and at times, you may feel like you just want to give up; life is not easy.

Believing that He will make your paths straight at a crossroad can be difficult when we are in the middle of a challenging situation or crisis. Trusting in what your eyes cannot see goes hand in hand with surrender of your will and holding onto His promises in faith. Especially when what you are trusting God for is delayed, do not give up through the tough times. There is a story in the bible about the angels fighting on our behalf and delay. I encourage you to read it yourself, but this part is from

> Daniel 10:12-13 NIV- *12"Then he said to me, "Do not be afraid, Daniel, for from the first day that you set your heart on understanding this and on humbling yourself before your God, your words were heard, and I have come in response to your words. But the prince of the kingdom of Persia was withstanding me for twenty-one days; then behold, Michael, one of the chief princes, came to help me, for I had been left there with the kings of Persia."*

God sent the angel in response to Daniel's words (prayers) that were heard but the angel was delayed because he was delayed in a spiritual battle.

Sometimes there is a delayed answer to our prayers that we wouldn't understand. Delay doesn't mean no. When you trust God and stay strong in faith, your blessings according to His will shall show up suddenly. God has a way of turning our disappointments into a setup for something better! During the most challenging times, push through and pray until something happens. Petitioning in prayer is your way to a breakthrough.

God loves you and wants you to show your trust in Him by talking about your feelings and circumstances with Him through prayer. God is not disappointed or frustrated by your struggles, doubts, or pain. He created you, knows you, cares about you, and you can trust Him with everything. When you want to stay spiritually fit, seek God and His Word for strength. Act in obedience, do what God says in His Word, and trust that He will take care of the rest. Do not look for security in other things; trust God to hold you securely through challenging circumstances.

> Philippians 4:13 NKJV- *"I can do all things through Christ who strengthens me."*

Answers to everything we go through in life can be found in the bible. There you will find strength and instructions to take care of yourself, protect yourself, love yourself, encourage yourself and others. God wants us to know about ourselves through understanding more about Him. After all, we are made in His image. Those who love God trust Him and walk through each day of life with a desire to know Him better. We have a choice, either to worry or to worship. God forgives you. Knowing this will heal you and help you trust that He is merciful and loves you. The more you pray, the more peace you will have. A heart at peace gives life to the body.

Before I knew who I was as a child of God, I let worry rule my life. I carried trauma around like a favorite pair of worn-out jeans. I had a victim mentality and sabotaged the good things in my life. Doing things my own way didn't make me happy. It took me a long time to figure this out and I didn't do it on my own.

I focused on the distractions in my life to avoid the truth. I was comfortable stuck in a rut because I unknowingly agreed with the lies the devil wanted me to believe. I needed to be healed and set free from soul wounds. Sin kept me connected with the demons and I didn't know who I was. Instead of seeking help, insecurity, offense, anger, and pain became my go to. How individuals react to a traumatic event, or an ongoing sense of danger depends on their trust and coping strategies.

Until I started seeking inner healing and learned to see myself how Jesus sees me, I was in bondage. I became conditioned to believe that living in darkness was my safe place. If you have found yourself in a similar place, you can find hope by leaning into God. When you do, you will learn that God is always right. I did not know what I was missing until Jesus set me free. I grew strong in my confidence in God and began to cut off people unworthy of my trust, who pushed my buttons, and triggered my trauma. I started reading the Bible and believing in what God says about me. I have willingly participated through years of emotional healing and deliverance. Jesus has given me the assurance of who I am, and that I belong to Him.

God *wants* you to know your Kingdom Identity, and how much He loves you.

God *wants* you to know your Kingdom Identity, and how much He loves you.

Things, situations, and trials of life will happen that are out of our control. But when we trust in God, stand on His promises, and believe what He says about us, we find peace. God gives us strength and fights our battles for us. Develop a plan and strategy to help you during those times when you might be tempted to give up. A plan will give you confidence in your ability to keep going. Trust that setbacks are a setup in your life for something better. Use uncontrollable situations as an opportunity to strengthen your faith and turn worries and cares over to Him. God's plans for you are always good ones.

We will not have all the answers, and we will not always understand why things happen the way they do, especially when things don't make sense. But, trusting in God gives us the freedom to focus on life's daily activities, knowing He has already got it all worked out for us. Peace and calm are a gift from the power of the Holy Spirit, but we have free will. The choice is ours, it is not always easy, but we do have the ability to control our emotions and not let our emotions control us.

His Word is unchanging and completely trustworthy. The Bible records ways God has responded to people through tough times in the past. It reminds us that He is faithful, no matter what our circumstances may look like.

The truth of scripture in the New Testament frees you from the expectations of earning your salvation. It also frees you from the unrealistic scenarios you may experience in everyday life. If you do not run to the Word of God to remind you of truth during challenging times, it is easier to be led astray by lies about your life that the devil wants you to believe. You need a solid foundation of scriptures to stand on, especially when you feel uncertain. Keep seeking God for answers then, you can cling to its truth when you face trials. When you trust God, you go to His Word when life is hard. You do not look for security in other things; you trust God to guide you through challenging circumstances. Act in obedience by doing what God says in His Word, and trust that He will take care of the rest.

> Psalm 37: 3-5 NIV- *"Trust in the LORD and do good; dwell in the land and enjoy safe pasture. Take delight in the LORD, and he will give you the desires of your heart. Commit your way to the LORD; trust in him and he will do this"*

Trusting in God means surrendering to His will. This will bring peace, joy, stability and put some gratitude in your attitude. No matter what, there's always a reason to find something to be grateful about. Trusting God is living a life in faith and obedience even when life is complex, and things may be complicated. The Bible tells us constantly to trust Him, especially when it is most difficult! When we trust God, we are saying He is dependable; we place our faith in His reliability.

When Jesus went to the cross, He took upon Himself the sins of the world, and His Blood is the ultimate sacrifice. When He died Jesus went into hell and took the keys from satan. Through His resurrection He gave us authority by the power of His name we can unlock the prison that once held us in bondage, and in Christ, we win.

Pray through the trials of this life. Perseverance helps build character. Just at that very moment when you feel like you cannot hold on any longer is when the miracle is about to happen, do not give up! Seek comfort in the arms of our loving heavenly Father. Imagine yourself in front of His throne and ask Him to hold you in His arms. Have confidence in the fact that you are sheltered under His protection.

> 1 Corinthians 10:13 NIV- *No temptation has overtaken you except what is common to mankind. And God is faithful; he will not let you be tempted beyond what you can bear. But when you are tempted, he will also provide a way out so that you can endure it.*

Temptations are common to mankind but God does not allow the devil to tempt us beyond what we can bear. When temptations of this world seem too much, He will provide an opportunity for you to remove yourself by giving you a way out. We are no longer captive to the fears that kept us in bondage or shackled by the chains of torment.

Jesus Himself felt overwhelmed by what was before Him for the sake of mankind, and He went straight to His Father. Knowing God will strengthen your trust in Him during times of hardship and the unknown. What I cannot do, *He can*. When I do not understand, *He does*, and *He will* when I will not.

He is the God of rest, peace, and comfort especially through the storms. Trust Him.

Chapter 5

Restoration of the Soul

Our soul is made of three parts: our mind, will, and emotions. When we surrender our soul to the leading of the Holy Spirit, we put on our Kingdom Identity. God wants to bring us to a place of surrender, totally dependent upon His leading. This is what is called a Spirit-led life. Most people live independently of the Holy Spirit every day. They never give it a second thought. We need to realize that the best decisions we can make are those led by the Holy Spirit and that walking in the spirit will have the best outcome for our lives.

In this season, God is restoring what the enemy stole, killed, and destroyed in your life and recovering the years you lost. So, allow Him now to restore *your* soul. If there is breath in your lungs, it's never too late to let God do a new thing in your life. He will cover you, protect you, and wants you to live a life filled with an abundance of joy!

Through Christ, we can do the impossible, and mountains must move because that's the kind of God we serve. What you have overcome, you now have authority over. God will use you to set captives free and anoint you to be a light in a dark place. I pray that you walk in an abundance of overflowing blessings in your life and receive all that God has for you. That the windows of Heaven will be opened over your life, and your blessings will be seeds that you bless others with.

Psalm 23:3 NIV- *"He restores my soul.He leads me in paths of righteousness for his name's sake."*

This is in the context of the Shepherd who leads His sheep to green pastures, quiet waters, and paths of righteousness. As Christians, we are the sheep in God's field, and only He can restore our souls. He transforms our mind, our will submits to Him, and our emotions don't dictate our attitudes or behaviors.

The soul is the deepest part of us and connects to our innermost being. Our identity is the Spirit of God, alive within us. Since God is the one who made us, only He can repair us because only He knows what we truly need to restore our souls and ignite our courage. When soul wounds are healed, you learn to shift your atmosphere with the light and love from God. Think of times past when God has saved you and healed you from unhealthy experiences that wounded your soul. He heals us and then gives us confidence in Him. He will do it again and again. Having your soul restored means you live out your identity, purpose, and destiny that you were created for.

God is the Almighty King of all the kingdoms, maker of Heaven and Earth, Creator of the Universe, and All that is in it. He is the way maker, miracle worker, promise keeper, light in the darkness, and no darkness will ever overcome it. Therefore, stay postured in His mercy with a humble yet expecting heart. Freedom is a part of your inheritance as a child of God.

God wants us to have boldness in Christ Jesus. When we starve fear and feed our souls with faith, we ignite a fire setting our souls ablaze, and hope becomes the oxygen that fans our flame. Our trust and hope develop into a supernatural lifestyle, and we grow stronger with time.

Many of us have been scorned by the enemy's lies and maybe from things we have seen or done. Shame tries to hold us back from God's-intended purpose for our lives. I am here to say to you, my friend, leave your guilt at the cross and rise with Christ because our old self has been washed away, and you are made new.

2 Corinthians 5:17- "*Therefore, if anyone is in Christ, he is a new creation. The old has passed away; behold, the new has come.*"

Your Past Is Not Your Future

You are no longer a victim of your past; you are victorious. You are continuously being reshaped by the hand of God. You are a champion, a kingdom warrior. Step into your destiny and walk confidently in your Kingdom Identity. You have been called out and set apart for His marvelous works. He chose you before the beginning of time and will transform you into who He created you to be, then use your past to show how mighty He is. Jesus, the eternal Son of God, born of a virgin, who lived a sinless life, loves us so much that He died for our sins. He became sin for us and took the punishment that we deserve, was buried, and on the third day rose from the dead. And I believe it. If you truly believe and trust this in your heart, receiving Jesus alone as your Savior, declaring, "Jesus is Lord," you will be saved from judgment and spend eternity with God in Heaven.

What is *your* response?

Yes, today, I decided to follow Jesus.

Maybe you are already a follower of Jesus but still have questions. Have you received Christ as your personal Savior? You can do it with me now. *Admit* you are a sinner and turn away from your sin. *Believe* Jesus Christ died on the cross to save you from your sins and give you eternal life. Ask Jesus to come into your heart. *Confess* that He is Lord and receive Him by faith.

You have been redeemed to move forward in a new life, and God is calling you to step into your destiny. The foothold the enemy thought he had over you has been bound up and cast into the depths of the sea. Our words have power. Speak prayers over your life that bring healing, confidence, strength, joy, and laughter. Declare the goodness of God over yourself and your family, finances, health, and give Him permission to rule and reign victorious over every part of your life. I encourage you to check out the Activation Prayer and Declarations in the back of this book.

Jesus has full authority over satan and the works of hell. As a born-again believer of Jesus, in His name, you have His authority to break chains of bondage, and every form of darkness must flee. God loves you, but it's your choice; you have been given free will to grab hold of your inheritance as sons and daughters of God. Exercise this right and walk in your authority. Knowing Your Identity in Christ *gives you the power* to take power and control away from the devil.

The heartbeat of Heaven is within the sound of your voice; shout into Heaven and Praise His Holy Name! Open the flood gates of Heaven and invite God by saying "*Let your goodness and mercy rain over my life, Lord.*" Ask Him now, "*Holy Spirit come like a rushing wind and fall like fire from the heavens over my life. In Jesus' name, I give myself to You Lord. I surrender!*"

God has given us the answers about restoring our souls in the Bible—the Word of God has the answers that give us understanding and wisdom to deal with everything we will ever face. It can make us wise unto salvation, serve to encourage us when we are faint-hearted, and be our guidebook to a life of peace and satisfaction. Although there are many great books written by men and women offering worldly wisdom, only God's Word is truly capable of restoring the soul and providing the truth and hope in times of distress.

Through the death and resurrection of Jesus, restoration of the soul is possible for those whose souls have been redeemed through faith in Christ. Jesus promised rest to all those who would come to Him, so we must be sure of our salvation and relationship with God. Only those truly born again in Christ can experience the fullness of peace and joy God has promised in His Word.

Thankfully, God provides for us when we face discouragement, trials, and temptations. He has provided us with primary sources of encouragement and strength. He has given us His Word to guide us, encourage us and nourish us spiritually. We need to spend time reading it, studying it with others, hearing it preached by men and women of

God, and most of all obeying it. God has also given us the privilege and power of prayer. We need to take our problems, discouragement, and tiredness to God in prayer, knowing He loves us and cares for us. He has given us other Christians to encourage and support us, but keep in mind that other Christians are only human.

Our praise opens doors for God to have His way in our lives. This strengthens us to walk boldly in confidence as God's children. The Word of God and prayer help us grow in our faith, refresh, and strengthen our souls. When we pray according to God's Word, it is our weapon of warfare. The Word of God is the food by which prayer is nourished and made strong.

I don't like to have anything get the better of me and take me out of my Godly character. You have all authority when the enemy tries to get a foothold in your life. We can be reminded of who we are by reading God's Word strengthens us to resist the devil and defeat the plans of darkness.

Do not allow the devil to lead you into sin by holding a grudge, nurturing anger, harboring resentment, or cultivating bitterness.

The enemy will lie to us to keep us in a place of bondage and unforgiveness. At which point, we lie to ourselves and begin to believe those lies. Some of us may even go through this in our own minds making excuses and blaming others for our behaviors.

Out of experience, I suggest that you keep in mind that you are not responsible for anyone else's healing but your own. Take responsibility and allow God to restore your soul no matter what anyone around you may be doing. I can promise you that if you change, then the people around you will have no other choice to change, or they will simply be removed from your life. Believe me, when I tell you, not everyone can go with you where God is taking you.

There is no need to try and prove anything to anyone, and at the end of the day, vengeance is God's. There's no need for payback. God will make everything work out exactly how He plans it when we are obedient to seeking His will for our lives.

When I looked inside and was honest, God told me loud and clear that it begins and ends with me. When I started seeking God asking

Him to restore my soul, He truly began to refine me from the inside out. I was no longer leaning on my own understanding but seeking God for guidance. We are written on the palms of His hands, and His nail scars are our names.

In Isaiah 49:16 NIV- *"See, I have engraved you on the palms of my hands; your walls are ever before me."*

His hands—His scars—*our names.*

We are protected by our God. The enemy's attacks can't get through when we guard our heart and mind in Christ. We have been separated, called out, set apart, and chosen. Our protection is forever and always, from God, through Christ Jesus, and our guidance comes from our helper, the Holy Spirit.

Character flaws such as pride rob us from allowing God to restore our souls. Kingdom greatness begins with being humble. We can be confidently humble, and pride is washed away when we begin agreeing with God's transformation by allowing Him to cleanse our soul through the water of the Word. Freedom is confidently knowing our Kingdom Identity and not needing to prove anything to anyone. We are loved, chosen, and understand who we are and belong to. This doesn't mean we are better than others, but what it does mean is that through God's grace and mercy, He has removed the veil allowing us to see what we didn't see before. You have been released from the entanglement of not seeing clearly. By reading the Word of God, it shows us how to live.

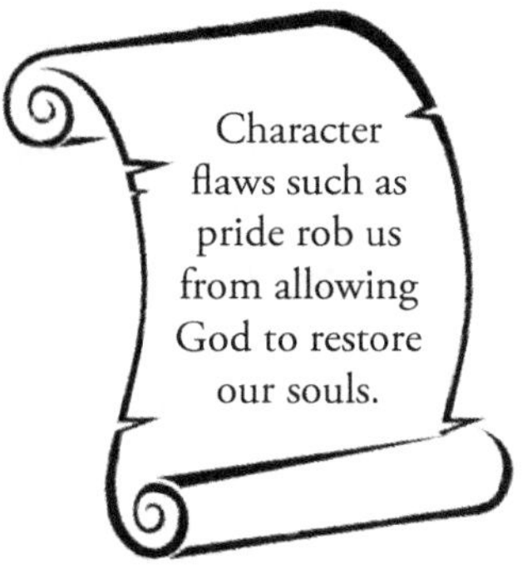

There are times when we all need an awakening, spiritual refreshment, and retreat for our weary souls. We feel alive when our souls are revived and refreshed. A healthy soul is continually strengthened and vigorous.

Remember your Kingdom Identity. Remind yourself daily of what God's Word says about you and remind yourself of who you are.

Remember the things that God has done in your life. Think back to the times He delivered you from bondage or sickness. How He provided for your every need and brought you through each trial. Remember that He is God!

> **Prayer-** "*Lord, help me remember the works you have done in my life. You are still God during seasons of drought and flourishing seasons, and you remain on the throne! Thank you for daily reminding me of your faithfulness through your Word. Amen.*"

Some days are better than others, and we may feel dry or burnt out at times. But God's Word refreshes us and gives us life.

> In Ezekiel 37:4-6 NIV, when Ezekiel witnessed the valley of dry bones, God spoke to him:
>
> *Then he said to me, "Prophesy to these bones and say to them, 'Dry bones, hear the word of the Lord! This is what the Sovereign Lord says to these bones: I will make breath enter you, and you will come to life. I will attach tendons to you and make flesh come upon you and cover you with skin; I will put breath in you, and you will come to life. Then you will know that I am the Lord."*

We can bring life and vitality to ourselves; there will be times you have to speak the Word of God to your own soul and prophesy over yourself.

> **Prayer-** "*Lord, help me to remember Who I am in You! I call on my memories of your goodness in my life. I speak words of Holy Ghost power into my soul. Refresh my soul Lord and give me the words to speak to the dry bones in my heart, give me the words to powerfully declare over myself and into the lives of others. Amen.*"

After Peter and John healed a lame man, Peter addressed the crowd that stood in amazement around them. Peter's message was simple:

Acts 3:19 NKJV- *"Repent therefore and be converted, that your sins may be blotted out, so that times of refreshing may come from the presence of the Lord."*

Here there is a connection. Spiritual revival and refreshment won't come until we repent from our sins and turn to God. Are there any areas in your soul that are dull and lifeless? Is there hidden sin buried deep within that you've suppressed and are hiding? Bitterness? Unforgiveness?

Jesus invites us to turn those things over to Him; it's time to leave it all at the foot of the cross and receive a refreshment for our souls.

Prayer- *"Lord, I repent of any unforgiveness and ungodly behavior in my life that does not honor and glorify you. Thank you that through Christ, I am forgiven, and I can experience revival and spiritual refreshment when I bring my worries and cares to you in prayer. Amen."*

Refreshing Others

Proverbs 11:25 NIV-

"A generous person will prosper; whoever refreshes others will be refreshed."

When we show mercy, grace, and kindness to those around us, we refresh others through love and humility. What we say to others and what we say to ourselves carries a lot more weight than we may realize. So, therefore, we must speak the life-giving, Spirit-breathed, refreshing wind of God to our souls and watch the dry valleys of our hearts break into floods of living water!

When we step out and meet the needs of others, we no longer wallow in the desolation that may be blocking us from walking in the fullness of God's truth, but we are refreshed by the many ways we can be a blessing to others.

When we do this, God gives us strength and we are revived when we reach out and refresh others with His flowing fountain of life. So, speak words of hope and healing to others and into your own soul today. Clothe yourself in garments of Christ's revitalizing splendor and find rest for your soul.

You will be revived, renewed, and completely refreshed!

Prayer- *"Lord, show me ways to refresh others by being a blessing to them. I know that I can experience your restorative power in my soul when I reach out to others with grace and love flowing through me. Amen."*

Revival in our world-first begins with the resurrected Christ in our own souls.

Chapter 6

Hearing and Obeying the Voice of God

John 10:27-29 ESV-

"My sheep hear my voice, and I know them, and they follow me. I give them eternal life, and they will never perish, and no one will snatch them out of my hand. My Father, who has given them to me, is greater than all, and no one is able to snatch them out of the Father's hand."

There are unlimited ways and times that God speaks to us. The question is, are we paying attention, and are we listening? Obeying God will give you the power to defeat the works of darkness. Speak with God through times of prayer and use the authority you have been given because of what Jesus did on the cross.

In previous chapters, we spoke about how God speaks to us through His Word and the Holy Spirit. God is God, and He will talk to us however and whenever He chooses. Just to name a few ways are through the Bible, other people, dreams, visions, and nature. The more in tune you are to hearing His voice, the more you will learn to recognize when He is speaking. The bible tells us that He will pour His Spirit on all flesh in the last days. I believe we are getting close to the second coming of

Christ and that we are living in exciting times of the last days. Some of the end-time prophecies in scripture have not yet been fulfilled, but I believe we're closer than we have ever been!

God wants us to enjoy our lives, He doesn't keep us on a leash, but sometimes we don't want to give Him the reins to guide our lives. We say we want God's will for our lives and may well intend to trust and desire God's guidance, yet we continually take back control and do things our way. Though we may give Him the reins to guide us, yet we sometimes fight with Him like a tug of war through disobedience when He tries to protect us, shield us, empower us, and guide us through our lives. When we are obedient to God's Word in the Bible, it won't lead us astray; we do that all on our own!

No matter what is going on in my life—I want to obey God no matter what it looks like. He needs us to participate; obedience will allow Him to do what He wants to do in us and through us.

> Exodus 19:5 NIV- *"Now if you obey me fully and keep my covenant, then out of all nations you will be my treasured possession. Although the whole earth is mine."*

Obedience to God's commands is the true sign of your love for Him, and the only way you can know if you are obeying God is by knowing His Word. Obedience is surrendering with the ability and strength to do what He asks while having the mindset and zeal to do those things.

To obey is better than sacrifice

Works of merit are not the same as obedience to God. Unlike the Law of Moses, which consisted of many sacrificial ceremonies with animal blood, specific rituals and symbols to remind the people frequently of their duties and responsibilities that when Jesus finally came among the Jews, they were in a state of profound apostasy. The "law" had become so corrupted with overzealousness that the original meaning of the ceremonial symbolism of the law of Moses was hard or even impossible to obey anymore.

Fortunately we have no other sacrifice than Christ to offer for our sins. However, our true faith in Christ is active in obedience. Don't allow yourself to be bound by religious traditions and man-made expectations. Don't limit your relationship with God to just going to church on Sundays, while that is a good thing, God doesn't live in a building, He is in you, and we are the church. The fruit of obedience is that it strengthens our beliefs and displays peace, honor, and joy even during our trials in life.

Stories of obedience occurred with plenty of the Bible's great individuals like Isaac, Joseph, Peter, Jesus, and His disciples. In the Bible it is recorded that through their obedience to God, they succeed in life. But, most of all, our gift of salvation is because of what Jesus did on the cross. All these stories of success, honor, and leadership are the outcomes of obedience.

Deuteronomy 11:1 NIV-*"Love the Lord your God and keep his requirements, his decrees, his laws and his commands always."*

The rewards of obedience are joy, peace, grace, and the abundant life that God wants for us. But, in disobedience, we are turning our fate over to the devil. When we align with Heaven and boldly step into our Kingdom Identity, it gives us all authority through Christ to defeat the enemy's plans. Part of that is paying attention to what we allow ourselves to listen to and believe in.

Psalm 23:1 ESV- *"The Lord is my Shepherd, I shall not want."*

If I ask God to have His way in my life and am obedient to where He's calling me and what He's telling me to do, He will make a way where there seems to be no way even when it may look impossible; just trust Him. Often, we don't associate the word obedience with a positive interpretation. However, the Bible tells us that obedience is for our own good. Obedience is meant to bring freedom and joy. It is a demonstration of a life surrendered to God at its essence.

I want to challenge your worldly definition of obedience and encourage you to align your heart to an understanding of the heavenly meaning. The Bible provides a complete guide for living life to the fullest, the best ways of treating others, identifying what's important, and prioritizing the things that matter most.

Let's touch on three points that will take us out of obedience

1: Distractions

There are three voices, God, Satan, my own voice.

When I don't know what to do, I call on God for confirmation. Especially with big life-changing decisions, unless I get confirmation, I'm not moving! God breathes on your prayers and the wind of confirmation from His mouth will give you new strategies and blueprints from Heaven to get to the promised land. The devil sends distractions that may look good in the moment to throw us off course.

There have been times I've lied to myself. I've tried to do things independently, even to the point of thinking I heard from God and then I wanted to take over and do it my way. Okay God, I heard you, thanks! I've got it God, now I can handle it from here. But, no baby, it doesn't work like that. Every time I didn't follow God's direction and follow it all the way through, I messed it up. I've discovered hard lessons and through these experiences, what we do, when and how we move forward are vital.

Busyness can be a distraction that delays what God has for our lives. Busyness does not equate productivity. When we are obedient to God's what, when, and how we are One with the Father, no one can snatch us away from His hand.

2: Lukewarmness

God is a gentleman. He's not going to force or invade His way into your life or make you submit and obey Him. His Spirit hovers and waits for your invitation. He gives authority to all who call on and abide in Him. When we abide in Christ, He becomes our comforter. Ask Him to show you His will for your life, get hungry for it!

In order to do God's perfect will, we must know what God's will is. This comes from a deep understanding of the scriptures and personal revelation from the Holy Spirit.

I can't emphasize enough the importance of studying the Bible. It's the key to a close relationship with God. Knowing His Word will not only comfort you in times of struggles but also serve as a guide to reaching your destiny! So, dedicate yourself to reading the Bible and get the truth of His Word rooted deep into your heart. Books like this one are great, but these are just a side dish of the Word of God. That's where you're going to hear God speak and see God move in your life. Read your Bible!

3: Selfish Desires

We literally need to shut our desires of the flesh up, it's a battle. We can't be of two minds. We can't believe in God's plans and will for our lives and then do it our own way. True disciples do it God's way, we need to overcome temptations and kill our selfish desires!

We must keep the helmet of salvation secure, tighten the belt of truth, and stay in the Word because it speaks to us. It's alive. Rivers of living water will flow into you and through you when you give Him your time, He will put His desires for your life on your heart. He wants to show up in ways you couldn't imagine.

Kingdom Treasures

God gave us instructions of righteousness to live by. He showed us the right path to live and gave us the instructions to pass down to our children and live productively in society. God's instructions teach mankind how to live right, treat others, love, forgive, and what to do; and not to do. These are Kingdom treasures.

Matthew 6:19-22 ESV-

"Do not lay up for yourselves treasures on earth, where moth and rust destroy and where thieves break in and steal, but lay up for yourselves treasures in heaven, where neither moth nor rust destroys and where thieves do not break in and steal. For where your treasure is, there your heart will be also.

"The eye is the lamp of the body. So, if your eye is healthy, your whole body will be full of light"

Our words are weapons, give your words an assignment and come into agreement with what God wants for your life. Words carry weight and we live in a voice activated kingdom. God created the heavens and the Earth with His words! Don't allow negative word curses to give permission to the demonic forces. God and the angels investigate our words and respond to our belief and obedience. The devil investigates our words as well and responds to our disbelief and disobedience.

John 8:31–32 ESV- *"If you abide in my word, you are truly my disciples, and you will know the truth, and the truth will set you free."*

One of the hardest things in life is to be obedient to God, especially when what He is telling you to do doesn't make sense. Whether it's a relationship, career, or life ambitions, sometimes God's plans for us are different than we might imagine or think we want. God can ask us to let go and trust Him so He can give us something better. By putting our hope in God's laws, though, under grace, we are confident and obedient to God's Word, the Bible. We base our lives on His truth and rely on it to guide us daily. Relying on God's Word means we are obedient to it. We want to follow Jesus because we have a relationship with Him.

As children of God, we desire to be in His presence and spend time with Him through prayer, worship and reading His Word.

Stay in communication with Him by seeking Him and knocking on the gates of Heaven.

> Matthew 7:7-8 NIV- *"Ask and it will be given to you; seek and you will find; knock and the door will be opened to you. For everyone who asks receives; the one who seeks finds; and to the one who knocks, the door will be opened."*

I left home at thirteen and wandered for twenty-two years selling cocaine to support my own cocaine addiction, was running numbers for the mob and involved in many other illegal activities. I was a career criminal, lived in darkness, I died while having surgery in a hospital and then came back to life on an operating table. But God still has a purpose for me, and for you no matter what we've done! Ask Him to show you your purpose according to His will, seek Him, and you will find it!

God has called me out of the grave, saved by His mercy and grace. I know He has a purpose and plan for each one of us. Many of us don't look like what we have been through, I understand scars run deep, yet God loves us, and He has called us according to His wondrous love.

No one can ever tell me God is not real, and until my last breath, I will tell of His Love and goodness to all who will listen. God uses our wounds to heal others and bring hope to those around us.

Green Pastures and Quiet Waters

> Psalm 23:2 NIV- *"He makes me lie down in green pastures; He leads me beside quiet waters."*

Sometimes life can take its toll on us. We become beaten down and weary without realizing it. During these times we are not nourishing ourselves to strengthen our soul. Maybe we are doing too much, and busyness becomes a distraction to wear us down.

God allows things in our lives to slow us down, and in those times when we cry out for Him, He slows us down enough to remember that we are His sons and daughters created to love Him first. Therefore, take time to rest in Him. God created us human beings, not human doings.

We are not perfect. Yet, though we fail, God looks at us through the loving eyes of Jesus! He leads us to green pastures and quiet waters to feed our soul through His Living Word.

I know from experience, it's in the broken places and most challenging times through life I've had to be still, call on Him, and wait on Him. He hears our cries, and He shows up! It may not be when we want Him to, but God is *always* on time!

The Right Path

> Psalm 23:3 NIV- *"He refreshes my soul. He guides me along the right paths for his name's sake."*

We find refreshment in the guidance and provision of our Shepherd. The refreshing paths in which God guides his sheep are the paths of righteousness.

For His namesake, we are called to share love with others. God takes a test of our lives and turns it into a testimony when we put our hope in Him. Sometimes, the disappointments we face in life are divine appointments for something better. God has a strategic way of setting us up and opening our eyes to see that the right path is in front of us, but we must allow Him to lead us.

> Psalm 23:4 NIV- *"Even though I walk through the darkest valley, I will fear no evil, for you are with me; your rod and your staff, they comfort me."*

We will face many trials in this lifetime: ups and downs, hills, and valleys. Walking through the valleys while on earth is part of the human experience. Sometimes life takes us through dark valleys where right paths feel wrong, and wrong paths feel right.

However, when we get out of our own feelings and seek His guidance, we can pass through the darkest of valleys without fear because we know our Shepherd is with us. He never leaves us, but we often turn away and think we can manage everything according to our own will. That is disobedience and allows the devil to trick us.

We're comforted to know that God is fully capable of guiding and sustaining us even when we get derailed. He puts us back on track when we seek guidance and comfort, through submitting our will and spirit to the Holy Spirit. There is comfort in following His lead, He won't lead us astray.

A Table in the Presence of Our Enemies

> Psalm 23:5 NIV- *"You prepare a table before me in the presence of my enemies. You anoint my head with oil; my cup overflows."*

The enemy at our table waiting to devour us can show up as anger, stress, frustration and other unhealthy emotions. God has prepared a table of peace, patience, kindness, love and joy for us in the presence of our enemies. He gives us the strength to overcome when we shift into a mind-set that we are victorious.

We are peace carriers of power, love, and sound mind in Christ Jesus. We are accepted and beloved. God wants us to live happy, joyous, and free. We are not slaves to our feelings; we stand upon the truth in the Word, and the truth sets us free.

God anoints our head with oil, meaning our thoughts, and hearts.

God wants to anoint your head with oil. He has an endless supply! His oil protects us, but we must protect the anointing and not waste our oil. Not everyone or everything is good for you, protect your heart and mind. The only thing that is guaranteed is that God loves you and

His plans are to prosper you no matter what circumstances surround you, obey God.

> **Prayer**- *"Thank you, Lord, for anointing my head with oil, I trust in You, my cup overflows with blessings."*

God's Goodness

> Psalm 23:6 NIV- *"Surely your goodness and love will follow me all the days of my life, and I will dwell in the house of the Lord forever."*

The Lord's goodness will be with us throughout our life.

He is faithful and His love will be present with you every step of your life's journey. Nothing can separate us from His love. God is good and doesn't send bad things to teach you a lesson. Bad things come from the devil but sometimes God allows it because He wants to get your attention.

Having the Lord as our Shepherd makes life worthwhile, we are blessed, and when our journey on earth ends, we will enter Heaven to live with our Shepherd forever.

> Revelation 7:16–17 NIV-promises that in heaven believers will never hunger or thirst or suffer again, *'Never again will they hunger; never again will they thirst. The sun will not beat down on them,' nor any scorching heat. For the Lamb in the midst of the throne will be their shepherd, and he will guide them to springs of living water, and God will wipe away every tear from their eyes."*

We are righteous and mighty in Christ Jesus and no weapon formed against us shall prosper. We are accepted into the family of Christ through His blood. The Lord is our good Shepherd, our Protector, our daily Provider, our Peace and Rest, and our Guide through every circumstance.

Remember All the Good Things

Ask God for the desires of your heart during times of prayer. Seek His thoughts, His heart, and His will for your life. Faith is confidence in things that we've not seen. When we keep knocking, believing and seeking, He answers our prayers. Don't give up!

All the good things that have happened in your life, focus on these things. Praise and worship God through song and dance. God sits on the praises of His people.

The Word of God is a prayer manual. Proverbs and the Psalms are full of them. When we pray according to God's will and word, *it will not return unto Him void!*

Obedience is surrendering to what, when, and what God wants for me. If it means I must wait for His confirmation while everyone else passes me by- then I will wait.

It's not easy to be obedient and wait on God
BUT
When confirmation comes, so do my wings.
When confirmation comes, so does my wind.

You will be blessed for your obedience, no one can take away what God has spoken over your life but you! This happens when we get out of the will of God and are not obedient to what He is asking us to do. When we give up, we are inviting the thief to take away what is rightfully ours.

His Image

God is the Potter, and we are the clay.

The clay is placed on a potter's wheel, and if it's not in the correct position the form will not take shape. Once the clay begins to take form, the clay needs water or else it starts to dry- Our water is the word of God.

Then there is the smoothing process, removing bubbles- this is transforming our mind, and renewing our hearts.

Once the clay goes into the fire and has been set, things can be placed inside.

Those things that are placed on the inside of you are your gifts and talents.

You are one of a kind!

Our purpose is revealed when we pray for God's will and seek His voice. God wants to mold and transform us, but we have free will, and for Him to do His best work, we must surrender our will and allow God to work in our lives. That means if I have a life-changing decision to make and God doesn't confirm it, I'm not doing it no matter how appealing it may be.

We live in a time and culture that places high value on appearances. A Lot of time and energy are wasted on keeping up the impression that we have it all together when not even one of us does. According to society our human confidence should be dependent on status quo and appearances. These are conditions and circumstances that are often unpredictable. No one always has it all together. Everyone has highs and lows.

Your confidence must be in Christ, then everything else will follow. By remaining surrendered to His will and allowing Him to shape every area of your life, you will be filled with confidence in the One who loves you more than anyone ever could. I call this Godfidence!

It's inherent in human nature to seek approval from others. It is a natural human tendency to rely on ourselves. Even Adam and Eve decided to do it on their own apart from God, and it is every human's natural first response. What's more, people and situations change, and things often happen beyond our control.

Prayer- *"God I am your clay. Mold me. I thank you for what You're doing in this season of my life. I draw closer to You in obedience while seeking Your will for my life. I declare victory over my life, and thank you for Your living water, that refreshes my soul. Amen."*

Chapter 7
Overcoming Temptation

God is the only steady, unchanging, altogether faithful and reliable entity. God alone is the uncreated One, the only self-existent and self-sustaining being. All good things are created and come from Him, and He is good down to His very essence. Trying to understand this is mind blowing!

He is the definition of the word '*good.*'

Therefore, God is worthy of all your trust, faith, and confidence in Him simply because of Who He is. God reveals Himself to us in His Word, and we are then transformed by the master's hands-on His potter's wheel.

He supernaturally intervened speaking through man for the recording of His words, wisdom, and guidance through the lives of men in the writing of scipture. He preserved it in the bible so we could have access to it throughout history and even today.

It's without error in its original manuscripts. The. Bible is the only thing that is holy, complete, and trustworthy. All things will pass away, but His Word will endure forever. The only thing that will not pass away is His Word.

You can confidently approach the God of the universe while resting in a humble assurance that He will receive you.

You are His.

You can have confidence in your salvation.

You can speak with God freely, constantly, without hesitation or reservation. He already knows everything about you. He loves you, is waiting for you to call on Him, and wants to hear from you.

The Lessons in Jesus' Temptation

Right after His baptism, and the Holy Spirit landed on Him like a dove, Jesus went into the desert for 40 days as a time of preparation for His ministry. Then Jesus was led by the Spirit into the wilderness to be tempted by the devil.

During the time in the desert Jesus was tempted by satan.

3 times in 3 different ways

The response and ways Jesus handled those temptations are examples of standing firm on God's word for strength, believing that God's promises are true, that He is a faithful God and will not leave or forsake us.

...

Physical Temptation

After fasting forty days and forty nights,

> Matthew 4:3 NIV- *The tempter came to him and said, "If you are the Son of God, tell these stones to become bread."*
>
> Matthew 4:4 NIV Jesus answered, *"It is written: 'Man shall not live on bread alone, but on every word that comes from the mouth of God.'"*

First

Jesus was hungry so the devil tempted Him with bread.

This was a physical temptation implying that Jesus should use His power for His own selfish purposes instead of God's mission. Satan's lie was that Jesus couldn't trust God, so He should take matters into His own hands. When faced with physical temptations, how often do we give in, and take matters into our own hands? We must be obedient to what God wants for us. This takes discipline.

Jesus' response was faithfulness to God, rebuking satan with God's word. The reward of your obedience will be an increase of God's favor and blessings in your life, even when it doesn't look like it during your trials. We gain authority in the areas that we overcome, and God blesses us to be a blessing to others.

The Emotional Temptation

Then the devil took Jesus to the Holy City and had Him stand on the highest point of the temple.

> Matthew 4:6 NIV- *"If you are the Son of God," he said, "throw yourself down. For it is written, "'He will command his angels concerning you, and they will lift you up in their hands, so that you will not strike your foot against a stone."*
>
> Matthew 4:7 NIV- *"Jesus answered him, "It is also written: 'Do not put the Lord your God to the test."*

Second

When satan invited Jesus to jump from a very high place to prove that He was the Son of God. The devil quoted a scripture passage to try and manipulate Jesus by using God's Words. The devil knows the bible and will try to use whatever he can to manipulate us. This was to entice Jesus into testing the Father's love for Him. Did the Father really love Him? The liar and thief satan tried to trick Jesus into making God prove His love for Him by putting Himself into harm's way and forcing God to help.

Jesus's response is firm and true to a timeless principle. Don't test God when He has already spoken clearly. God the Father loved Jesus, as He made clear when God spoke from the heavens on the day of His baptism.

> Matthew 3:17 NIV- *"This is my son, whom I love; with him, I am well pleased."*

I have put myself in harm's way many times in my life, although it wasn't a test of God's love. It was because I didn't know how to love myself. But no matter what, God always showed up to protect me when I called on Him. If you look back on your life, do you remember all the times God showed up for you? God always protects those who call on Him.

If you look back on your life, do you remember all the times God showed up for you?

It may not be the way we want Him to, but He continually shows up.

The Temptation of Control

Again, the devil took Him to a very high mountain and showed Him all the kingdoms of the world and their splendor.

> Matthew 4:9 NIV- *"All this I will give you," the devil said, "if you will bow down and worship me."*

Matthew 4:10-11 NIV- *Jesus said to him, "Away from me, Satan! For it is written: 'Worship the Lord your God and serve him only." Then the devil left Jesus, and angels came and attended to Him.*

Third

Satan tempted Jesus with a promise to take over the throne in an attempt to deceive Him by offering control over all the world's kingdoms if He worshiped him.

Though satan, once an exalted angel of God's Kingdom, was cast out of heaven, he insultingly suggests that he is worthy of worship. The accuser and liar said, you need only to worship me. This was to imply that Jesus could take a shortcut to fulfill God's purpose. All the world's dominion would be given to Jesus when He finished His work but not before. His assignment involved crucifixion and His blood is the ultimate sacrifice.

Before Jesus could sit on the throne in Heaven, He had to hang on the cross. Jesus came to the earth for God's Kingdoms, to draw all man unto Him, take back the keys and authority from satan, and give it to those who believe in and call on the name of Jesus.

Jesus is in heaven seated at the Father's right hand, interceding on our behalf against the accuser satan.

Anything satan has to do with is wicked in all ways and leads to destruction. He tempts us with things that may make us feel good for a little while but indeed lead to destruction, darkness, and death. When our soul is dark, we are sick; it is the same as living life as walking dead. In the end, we miss knowing who we were created to be. We see that satan threw his best shot at Jesus, and how Jesus handled these temptations with God's truth are instructive ways for us to follow.

Resist the Devil and He Will Flee from You

No one is exempt from temptation. Not even Jesus was. The key to this is that He resisted. There is no reason to think that you or I will be spared, so don't be surprised when temptation comes. Temptation is not the same as sin. It is not a sin to be tempted or to feel temptation. Temptations expose weaknesses we may have knocking at our door. Jesus was tempted, but He never sinned. It becomes a sin when we take the bait.

Respond to temptation with God's word and the truth - *It is written.*

You are an overcomer and can do all things through Christ. James 4:7 NKJV- *Therefore submit to God. Resist the devil and he will flee from you.* Do not entertain the devil. Resist him and he will *flee.*

If you have a particular area that satan uses to tempt you, defeat it with God's Word. Memorize a Bible verse that deals directly with that temptation. God's Word will not come back void. It is our weapon!

God calls us to remain loyal to Him because of who He is. The One who rules and reigns above all, the Alpha and Omega, the beginning, and the end.

God's mercies are new every morning, and He knows you better than you know yourself. Responding to temptation with the truth from God's Word breaks the lies from the devil and gives us strength. Resist the devil, pursue the will of God for your life and keep believing. You are an overcomer!

Jesus has experienced life as a human man. He experienced temptation, sorrow, and heartache. He understands how we feel and what we face in life. God wrapped Himself in the flesh and came to earth as a man who then gave Himself as the ultimate living sacrifice so that we could be free from the wages of sin and death.

You don't have to live in fear that you will lose the gift of salvation that He gave you.

You don't have to hope that you'll be saved or think maybe you'll go to heaven at the end of your life or that you didn't do enough to be saved. It wasn't given to you by works, but by the grace of God, you could never do anything to earn it and could never do enough to keep it, it is God's gift.

If you believe in Christ, that He died in your place to reconcile you to God and that He paid for your sin with His life, then you are sealed by the blood with His gift of salvation. That's the beauty of His work.

If good works can't earn your salvation, and good works aren't a guarantee of your salvation, then what are good works in the Christian life?

Good works flow from your salvation because of your Kingdom Identity in Christ. They are a manifestation of your new life in Christ. After receiving salvation, God begins to draw you near to Him and transform you to be more like Him.

He changes your ways, transforms your mind, gives you a new heart, and invites you into the work He's already doing all around you. But now He wants to live in you, work through you, and requires that you have confidence in following Him. God wants you to be a vessel of His goodness and share His love with those around you. The work of the Christian is to love God first and love others.

Find your confidence in Christ. God will never change. Though He is always doing something new, His Word, mercy, and grace will never change. Humble yourself, and He will lift you up. When we love God and allow Him to work in our lives, He will work all things for our good. Freedom and confidence in Christ are gifts available to all because He loves us, we could never earn it, and God doesn't expect us to. He knows you will never get it all right. He is a God of love. His mercy and grace flow freely when you ask for forgiveness and repent when you mess up along the way.

God is not a God of condemnation who wants us to be held in bondage of shame or guilt. The devil is a liar and will try to hold you in the bondage of sin using shame and guilt against you. Jesus took on all your sins past, present, and future at the cross.

God is, however, a God of conviction. Conviction is not the same as shame or guilt, and it's not knowledge of right and wrong. Simply put, conviction is that we are concerned, mindful, and possibly grieved about how our sin dishonors God because our hearts desire is to honor and please Him. When we mess up, His mercies are new every morning. Don't live your life asking for forgiveness over and over for something He has already forgiven you for.

Praise and worship glorify God; however, it has become the focus in many Churches. The lights, the popularity of leadership, clicks within groups of people, making the Pastor an idol. The church isn't a building on Sunday. It is Jesus inside of you- We are the church. Many people have lost sight of the true reason for going to church on Sunday, for some it's become a social club. Church is a place where we can enjoy community, use our gifts, discover our purpose, learn the word, practice generosity and be around Kingdom Family. Fellowship with other believers is critical because we are stronger together. But when we lose focus, we are in a system of religion and not in a relationship with God.

Our confidence needs to remain in Him. Ultimately, God will have the last say. He assures us that those who remain steadfast will be victorious and ultimately delivered from the troubles in the end times.

Through Jesus, we have been saved by grace to glorify God and love others. Kingdom Identity is rooted in knowing who we are, and who we belong to. It's seeing the gold in everyone, especially those who may not know who they are yet.

God needs our faith to be rooted in the teachings from His Word. All things are made by God and created for God. We must depend entirely upon Jesus and remember that without Him we have nothing, but with Him we have everything.

When you don't have Christ you have no power over sin, death or satan's tricks and temptations, and you won't live your life to the fullest that God intended for you.

The increase of confidence in Christ comes through our daily trials, struggles and in our brokenness when we seek Him in everything. Strength and sharpening begin by believing in who God says we are.

To gain full confidence in Christ we must be willing to give up some things in exchange for what God calls us to do. We must have an unshakeable faith and inner determination to stand firm on what He is telling us to do. Jesus was hungry, but He would rather be hungry than abuse His power in something God hasn't told Him to do.

What are you using your power on? Are you trying to manipulate something to work out the way you want it, or are you submitting that power to God and surrendering to His will? Jesus submitted His power to God, and God raised Him Up to be glorified by All men and women. Even the birds, the creatures, the stars and all of creation worship God.

When you are faithful to God with the little things you have been given, He increases your blessings because He knows He can trust you.

I do my best to submit my gifts, time, energy, and mind to be used for God.

My mind doesn't always want to do what God wants me to do; my mind doesn't always want to make the right decisions. Because of this, I must submit my mind, will, and emotions to God, and ask in prayer-

"How do You want me to use these gifts, God?"

"What can I do with what You've given me to glorify You?"

It's then I receive increased confidence in Christ to do things that will please Him.

There is much more God wants to trust you with. Are you willing to go hungry before you abuse what God has given you? This is a mind-set that is not an easy task, but if you are willing to be obedient to what God wants for you, God will multiply your abilities to do things in a way you could never do on your own.

In John 14:12 NIV- Jesus says, "*Very truly I tell you, whoever believes in me will do the works I have been doing, and they will do even greater things than these, because I am going to the Father.*"

You and I have been called upon by God to pray for the lost, feed the hungry, lay hands on the sick, and even raise the dead. Jesus raised the dead and He said if we believe in Him, we will do even greater things than He did. God is calling you towards Him and wants to give you His power to reach the lost and broken, to turn their hearts to Him. - Will you answer the call?

Chapter 8
The Power of Forgiveness

Forgiveness is a choice.

You might have experienced things that were not your fault, but you are responsible for your healing. You are not defined by your past no matter where you've been, what you've done, or what has been done to you.

Part of the healing comes through forgiveness. You may think it's impossible to forgive someone, especially if they have no conscience or have no consequence for the wrongs they have inflicted. When someone has hurt or disappointed you, the logical response would be to think that you're hurting them by not forgiving them and holding a grudge.

You are causing yourself more pain by holding on to anger, and you have given the person that you wish not to forgive power to control you. However, you can get that power back when you forgive.

Forgiveness does not condone someone's behavior, but it releases us from our own mental prison. By forgiving the person or people who hurt us, we are set free! We find the freedom to experience peace and tranquility.

Forgiveness is not approving or justifying what happened. God forgives people but disapproves of their sin, so we also need to understand that forgiving someone doesn't justify wrongdoing. Jesus forgave the woman living a life of adultery, but He disapproved of her behaviors. He told her to leave her life of sin. Forgiveness does not require us to call a wrong a right. Justification for wrongdoing is a trap from the devil; forgiveness does not mean we are to excuse destructive behaviors.

Reconciliation and forgiveness are not the same. Forgiveness does not mean that we pretend we weren't hurt, nor does it require that the offender gains access to us again. Sometimes the healthiest thing is to forgive without allowing the offender access to you. It is excellent to restore a relationship but that takes agreement from all involved and shouldn't be pressed. Maybe you don't want to see the person who wronged you, or perhaps they don't want to see you.

Sometimes forgiveness is loving people from a distance. Love doesn't erase our memories. When we are fully aware of the wrongdoing and choose to show grace in forgiveness, it demonstrates God's love for us. God doesn't forget our sins; He desires to overlook them because He loves us and chooses not to remember them, so our sins are not held against us. Even though we may not be able to forget wrongs that have been done to us, we must not dwell on them.

Forgiveness doesn't mean we aren't hurt by things that happen, nor does it deny what happened.

Suppressing what happened to us is harmful and is often done unconsciously. Unfortunately, this doesn't remove a wound; it only puts it on the back burner and more times than not will surface as a trigger from something else that manifests in unhealthy ways. It will often occur, causing high blood pressure, anxiety, panic attacks, irritability, or in some cases worse.

We need to manage our lives from a place of total forgiveness, and it is not possible by repressing harmful events. True forgiveness is coming to terms with the reality that wrongs have been done. There is freedom and victory that comes from facing the problem for what it is, understanding the seriousness of the offense, and still choosing to forgive. To forgive we must look unclouded at the wrong we are forgiving and understand its seriousness. Forgiveness does not mean we are oblivious to what has happened. Nor is it making excuses for the offender or covering it up, that is denial. Someone who is trying to forgive an offense but pretends that it never happened by denying or repressing the event is a trap that leads us into a vicious cycle of abuse.

Sometimes people feel that if they forgive an event, they are turning a blind eye or ignoring the wrongdoing. Willful blindness is a conscious choice to pretend that a situation never happened, unlike denial or repression. When we try to forgive an offense but pretend that it never happened, we will eventually explode. Often, we can become an offender or abuser because we did not deal with the pain the original offense caused. Forgiveness doesn't pretend that nothing happened.

It is hard to let go of the desire to make them pay for or get them to admit what they have done, especially knowing that they are getting away with what they did and that no one will ever know what they have done. But when we face the truth of the offense and accept in our hearts that we can't control another person, only ourselves, we are free to release the bondage and self-torment that comes with the desire to make them pay for what they did. When we bless and release them from the retaliation we want for them, we release our desire for revenge because of their wrongdoing.

In the Bible Deuteronomy 32:35 NIV God says:

> *"It is mine to avenge; I will repay. In due time their foot will slip; their day of disaster is near and their doom rushes upon them."*

We are called to trust God and our position is to be a pure and submissive heart unto Him. As we obey and trust Him, we grow in faith. Our God is a God of Justice. We are to pray for our enemies and bless them; maybe your enemy is those who have hurt you. To get over what someone has done to you, you must pray about it and let go of it. Release them, and you will be released. The bondage that comes with staying angry isn't worth holding onto unforgiveness. Don't allow the rocks of negativity and unforgiveness to weigh you down.

Let me be clear; *the lack of peace isn't worth it.* There is a sense of inner peace, rest, and clear thinking when we choose to forgive.

We create new memories of pleasant thoughts. These are all available to you, but you must let go of resentment to experience them. Who knows how God will use you to help others if you set your enemies free and never look back?

> Matthew 6:15 NIV- *"But if you do not forgive others their sins, your Father will not forgive your sins."*

This doesn't mean God doesn't love you or that He won't guide and look after you. When I didn't forgive others who have wronged or hurt me, I was blocking the blessings God had for me. I couldn't step into the fullness of life because of the bitterness I carried. I lost time and wasted energy dwelling on things I couldn't change instead of doing something about what was available to me to make a change within myself. The refusal to forgive leads to many people's mental, emotional, and physical self-harm. Common mental health and emotional issues associated with unforgiveness, and resentment are drug or alcohol abuse, depression, anxiety, short-temperament, hostility, hatred and sleeplessness. Forgiveness helps you manage stress.

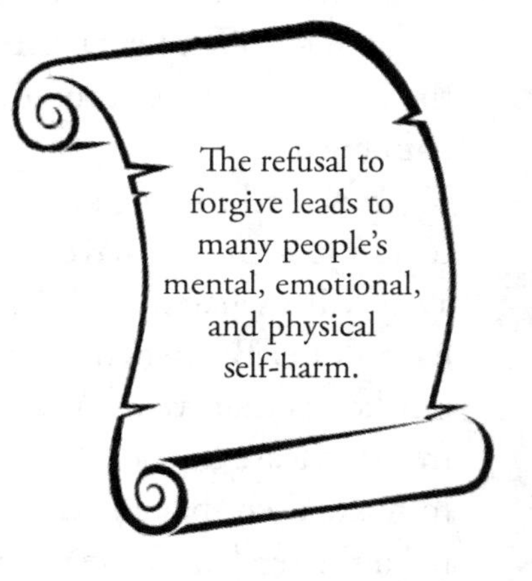

Unforgiveness is when you are unwilling or unable to forgive someone for hurting, betraying, breaking your trust, or causing intense emotional pain. Unforgiveness partners with worry, it is aging and puts lines on faces before they should come. For some, it brings sleeplessness; in others, it can trigger high blood pressure or even a heart attack.

Lack of forgiveness makes it easy and natural to be a bitter person while feeling no conviction that it is wrong to carry resentment. Whether you're working on forgiving yourself or others, forgiveness is imperative for mental and physical health.

When I was holding onto anger and resentment, I missed hearing from God and walking into all he wanted to give me in life. As a result, I forfeit the freedom and happiness that could have been mine all along. The consequences of an unforgiving spirit are countless.

The devil does not want you to forgive others, he loves when you are bitter. This is a way he has access to you. He will give you what appears to be good reasons for you to hold on to your resentment and for your abuser to be punished.

Internal conversations about putting the person in their place are motivated by the devil. He wants to rob you of your time, energy and joy. When we try to forgive, he will put obstacles in our path and give us every opportunity and reason not to forgive. He comes to rob, kill and destroy any areas of happiness we are stepping into for our future.

Unforgiveness is a stronghold that we must be broken free from. Dismantle the old thoughts and replace them with new ones. When we remove the bitterness and replace it with God's truth, we can take our thoughts captive in obedience to see ourselves as Christ sees us. You must release your offender into the hands of God. Our God is a God of Justice. Sometimes seeking revenge will land us in worse situations. It can bring destruction to your relationships. We must not take matters into our own hands to get even with those who have hurt us. Bitterness, resentment and anger want us to take matters into our own hands. Forgiveness trusts that vengeance is the Lords.

Sometimes our lives can be shaped because of things that have happened to us, or maybe the choices we made. Sometimes we build walls and develop unwanted behaviors to push people away to avoid getting hurt. Perhaps you've lived through trauma and don't want to let others in because of past hurts. Maybe you can't get close or trust anyone out of fear of getting hurt. You may even believe that the shell and wall you've built is to protect you and it's who you've become, but that isn't the real you that God created. When we choose not to forgive, we give the offense a legal right to continue to cause us pain and suffering.

This builds resentment and develops when you hold a grudge and become inwardly bitter. You become preoccupied with hate. By doing this you have opened the door, given the devil a piece of your heart and given bitterness a right to stay. But as a born-again believer, you have the authority to shut the door and lock it by releasing yourself through forgiveness. Ask yourself what lie has the enemy said that you believed and is causing you to hold on to unforgiveness? Bitterness is a root that must be pulled out. You must deliberately ask God to remove the bitterness, and this means you can no longer justify your resentment.

Our personal responsibility is not to depend on blaming others for our anger, resentment, or bitterness. Sometimes we may need to forgive ourselves. Maybe you are justifying your bitterness because of shame or guilt. Shame is when you tell yourself there is something terrible about you. Guilt is that you did something terrible that you can't let go of. Condemnation keeps us in bondage, but the bible tells us that there is no condemnation in those who are in Christ Jesus. The Lord is the Spirit, and where the Spirit of the Lord is, there is freedom. There is a battle over your identity and destiny. Fear, condemnation, shame, and guilt will paralyze you and stop you from stepping into your future and revelation of Christ. Your Kingdom Identity is a supernatural revelation of the spirit. When the word of God penetrates your heart, it washes over your mind and revelation of truth occurs. You gain confidence and freedom based on supernatural revelation. If you haven't started already, I encourage you to begin speaking with God through 2-way journaling, with what you are saying and write what you hear God saying to you. Writing also helps to get rid of any negative suppressed emotions.

Jesus died at the cross for all our sins, He doesn't want us to carry guilt or shame they need to be left at the cross. You need emotional heart healing if you think you must suffer because of something you've done. This will help you see yourself as Jesus sees you. Sometimes the hardest person to forgive is ourselves. Sometimes it's easier to blame others for causing you pain. However, the depth of the pain depends on the boundaries that you set within all your relationships. Forgive yourself for allowing others to treat you with disrespect or emotional pain. Spend time with God and ask Him what He wants you to repent from. Repentance is to turn from sin and dedicate oneself to the amendment of one's life, to feel regret, to change one's mind. Then ask God to forgive you. This is difficult because the devil doesn't want you to forgive yourself. He wasn't to keep you locked in the bondage of shame and guilt. He wants you to believe you are not worthy of God's forgiveness. Take those thoughts captive because they are not from God, and they are not yours. They are thoughts from the kingdom of darkness to keep you in bondage until you believe that you are defeated. Shame leads to self-pity, and this will paralyze you from walking into your Kingdom Identity. Tell those thoughts to leave and that you are God's child forgiven and loved. Jesus gave His life and paid for your sin against yourself and others, all of it is covered!

Religion makes us work harder to earn God's love, but because of Jesus, we can have a relationship directly with God. And He loves you, He forgave you, forgive yourself. Even though you forgive yourself, there may be people who don't want to forgive you. That is not your responsibility to make them forgive you. Pray for their healing and keep stepping into all God has for you. People sometimes have a tough time seeing that you are a new person and are not the same. They may even want to keep you in bondage by using your past against you. But keep this in mind, it is not coming from them it is the spirit of darkness working through them to try and hold you in that prison of shame and guilt. Maybe you need to distance yourself from these relationships if they are unhealthy relationships.

Undealt with anger, resentment and bitterness can manifest a critical spirit. Without even realizing it you may become critical of others. Taking the focus off ourselves, we begin pointing the finger at others. It's been said that a little bit of knowledge can be a dangerous thing. Sometimes being a little bit spiritual can be hazardous because it can give us just enough self-righteousness to look at what's wrong with others. Criticism is uncalled for, and it is hurtful. It's not our place to tell someone what's wrong with them and what they need to change about themselves. These conversations are counterproductive, and they grieve the Holy Spirit. When you lose your rationality and aren't thinking clearly, you may lose your self-control. All hell can break loose when you don't control your tongue. You don't want to do or say anything out of a critical spirit that you will be sorry for later. The only ones we can change are ourselves. The actual test of spiritual maturity is to overlook what we think is wrong in others and see their good. When you ask God to come into your life and forgive you, He will. But if you begin pointing the finger criticizing and judging others, four fingers are pointing back at you. The urge to criticize others comes from a place of feeling devalued and is a defense mechanism to relieve our own insecurities. More times than not, critical people were criticized by someone they trusted to take care of them as a child. This can be traumatizing and the need to forgive the person or persons who hurt you will give you patience and tolerance. Forgiveness of those who hurt you will also increase the acceptance of yourself and others imperfections. We are often most critical of something we see in others that we don't like about ourselves.

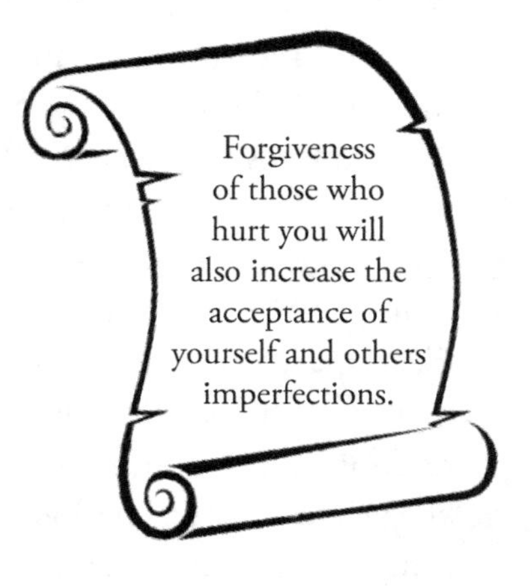

We are at war and our weapons of warfare are not related to physical, they are spiritual and we are fully equipped for spiritual battle through the word of God. When we continue walking in covenant with God He fights our battles for us, gives us purpose, and establishes us in Him to show others how powerful He is. We are to be a lighthouse for others to see that God also loves them. Your value doesn't come from what you do, it is in who you are as a person.

We are strengthened through humility, a humble attitude that expresses itself in the patient endurance of offenses. This is a controlled strength; we learn to not react to others but to respond with love. Sometimes the best response is no response at all. The way to take responsibility is to allow the Holy Spirit to lead. By culture, powerful usually means the loudest person in the room but powerful people are in control of themselves, they are not boastful, arrogant or proud. They show respect and don't try to control others. Powerful people don't try to make others respect them; they are respected because they show respect.

They are not affected or infected by their environment, and they refuse to be sucked into other people's drama. Powerful people require the people they surround themselves with to be powerful. They create powerful people around them wherever they go. Powerful people see in others what their potential is. When they encounter a person who carries a lesser power, they don't jump in and try to be someone's lifesaver, they are not manipulating or condescending.

Powerful people take responsibility for each day and always connect with the Father in heaven before starting the day. Their love towards humankind is not dependent on people liking them. Their choice to lead in love to those around them stands no matter what another person says or does. Powerful people are who they say they are in their actions and lead by example. They create a safe place for others to be known and speak positivity and encouragement into the lives of others. They create a safe environment and accept others while encouraging them to be themselves versus an unsafe environment where people must perform to be accepted.

Powerful people make daily decisions that align with a dream or vision and respond to build and bring it to life. They speak positively because they know their words create the world around them that makes their tomorrow. Powerful people let their yes be yes, and their no be no. They know how to love others without expectations, especially showing kindness to those who can do nothing for them.

Powerful people forgive themselves and forgive others.

End Word

For me, there is no turning back; I'm not perfect, none of us are but I do my best to live a Kingdom lifestyle. I now walk in confidence to do God's work until my last breath, and I'm called home, where I will spend eternity in heaven.

My family needs me to do this, my daughter needs me to do this, future generations need me to do this, and most of all, God needs me to do this because I am His hands and feet here on earth and *so are you!*

Thank you for reading. I hope you were moved by this book, please share it with at least one person that God puts on your heart.

I thank God for each of you and am praying that you will know the freedom that is only available through Jesus. I am interceding for you and love you dearly.

Trust the Lord with all your heart and lean not on your own understanding. In all your ways submit to Him and He will make your paths straight.

We are created for His great pleasure and to have a relationship with Him.

In all you do, do for the Glory of God, and you will prosper.

God Bless you and yours,
In His Service
Lisa Ann

Appendix A: Prayers

If you have read this far and are hungry for more, I invite you into an activation prayer.

This prayer was inspired by and cited with permission from the Activation Prayer in the book Supernatural Freedom from the Captivity of Trauma by Dr. Mike Hutchings Director of Global Awakening School of Supernatural Ministry.

Many of you have gone through life not knowing who you are or your purpose. I believe maybe you've been looking for answers for a very long time but didn't know where to turn. I encourage you to speak this over yourself and receive a breakthrough and healing touch from the Hand of God.

> *"In the name of Jesus, we thank you Lord for sending the Holy Spirit right now to this reader. The Holy Spirit is with you as your comforter, your friend and the one who knows everything you've been through. He is not here to expose you or hurt you or traumatize you in any way. Instead, God is here to heal you and take the shattered pieces of your broken heart and put them back together again. He is here to restore you and give you a life of freedom and purpose so that you can walk out in peace all the days of your life. He is eager to cast off the false identity you have been struggling with and reveal your true God-given identity, your kingdom identity as a son or daughter because God has wonderful plans for you."*

Jeremiah 29:11 NIV

"For I know the plans I have for you," declares the Lord, "plans to prosper you and not to harm you, plans to give you hope and a future."

God's Invitation

God is inviting you into a safe place right now even though it may not feel safe at times. Perhaps this is because of the things that will try and trigger you. Be assured that God is with you, and He has defeated the enemy of your soul on the cross through His son Jesus Christ. The enemy has no power to undo the cross. Jesus has all authority, and it has been given to Him by God the Father. Any discomfort you may feel is the feeble attempt of a defeated foe to remain in control over your life. Right now, by the power of the blood of Jesus I welcome the Holy Spirit to come upon you as your comforter, helper, healer, and deliverer.

I declare the forgiveness, love, mercy, and grace of God over your mind, body and soul in Jesus' name. No matter what you have done or what has been done to you, you are free and no longer defined by your history and past. You are now defined by who your God calls you to be, His beloved child.

By the power of the blood of Jesus I break the lies of shame or guilt you may carry due to any trauma or traumatic experience. What was done to you or what you have experienced does not speak to who you are. You no longer carry shame because none of God's children have shame. I break the power of guilt that you carry for sin or things you did to cope with your pain. In the name of Jesus there is no condemnation. The law of the spirit of life has set you free from the law of sin and death.

By the power of the declaration of Isaiah 61 I declare the spirit of the Lord God is here to bring the good news to your broken heart. He is here to heal you and declare liberty and freedom. Right now, he is bringing comfort from mourning, joy for sorrow, a mantle of praise for the spirit of heaviness through divine exchange and giving you beauty for ashes. I sever every single assignment of the evil one against you. In the name of Jesus, I command spirits of trauma, torment, and fear, to leave now in the name of Jesus. I severe your assignment against this person by the power of the blood of Jesus Christ. Spirit of suicide, I break your power now and I command you to stop speaking right now. I speak to murder and rage, and I sever your assignment in the name of Jesus you no longer have a place in the life of the person that is reading this. I sever right now the spirit of death. I say to you reader that you carry the same spirit that raised Jesus's body from the grave. I command the spirit of death to leave you now in Jesus' name. I cancel and break off addiction, depression, oppression, insanity, mental illness, and the spirit of bipolar or multiple personality disorders in Jesus's name. I sever your assignment from the person reading this in Jesus' name.

Now I sever the spirit of lust, perversion, sexual violation, and slavery off the one reading this in Jesus's name. I declare that chains and shackles of sexual perversion and lust are broken off you in Jesus' name. You are no longer in any way, shape, or form under the thumb of sexual perversion. I break the power of pornography. I sever the hold it has upon your soul and mind. I command the images and memories of pornography to dry up and die right now.

I invite you to put your hands on your heart as I speak, healing to your broken heart in Jesus's name. Let the power of the Holy Spirit come now to pick up the pieces and put them back together so you can walk in freedom knowing your true Kingdom Identity. You are God's child, and, in His grace, you are stepping into everything you were created to be and do. I declare that as healing comes to your heart, the shalom of God that brings wholeness and wellness will affect your mind, will, emotions, and your body in the name of Jesus.

I invite you to put your right hand on your head, in the name of Jesus, I speak to every traumatic image and memory in the right lobe of your brain and command these images to dry up and die. I sever the neuropathway that leads to these dramatic images and memories. I sever your seeing, smelling, tasting, touching, and hearing from being triggered Through these neuropathways. I sever every lie and stronghold connected with traumatic images and memories. I pray for fresh faith and the truth of the word of God to replace those lies and images and memories. I command the memory center to wake up, wake up, wake up sleeper, wake up!

Let there be a free flow of memory from the memory center of your being so that what is restored to you are good memories about your life. Your mind is no longer held captive or hijacked by traumatic images and memories. I speak healing to any concussions, traumatic brain injuries, or anything that has caused your brain not to operate in the way it was originally intended by God. I command rewiring of the brain and proper neuro function in the name of Jesus. I break the diagnosis of ADHD, dyslexia, loss of cognitive function in the name of Jesus.

I pray healing over auditory and visual processing in the name of Jesus. I command any masking of trauma that looks like mental illness that was really caused by trauma to be healed in the name of Jesus. I declare healthy functions and connections be restored between the right and left lobe of your brain. I declare the right lobe completely restored and healed right now by the power of the blood of Jesus Christ. We thank you for doing it Father.

I speak to all systems of your body and their functions be healed now in the mighty name of Jesus. I speak to your nervous system that includes your eyes and your ears, your brain and spinal cord and your nerves and command them to be healed. All chronic nerve pain must leave now in the name of Jesus. I command the endocrine system consisting of your network of glands that release and regulate your homeowners to be set back into its original settings so that all glands operate properly with the right flow of hormones in the name of Jesus.

I speak to your musculoskeletal system consisting of your muscles, bones, cartilage, and ligaments and declare every memory from a traumatic event be released now from muscles and other areas so that all pain associated with accidents in our area so that all pain associated with accidents and ungodly touch between humans is removed and replaced by the peace and shalom of God.

I speak healing to your circulatory systems consisting of your heart, blood vessels, and lymphatic system and declare healing and Jesus' name.

I speak to your urinary tract system consisting of your kidneys, bladder, and related ducts and declare them heels and restored in the name of Jesus.

I speak healing to all aspects of your digestive system consisting of your mouth, esophagus, stomach, and bowels, and declare it healed so that you are able to eat of the healthy foods on God's earth has he intends and that you digest them well so that they nourish and sustain your body all the days of your life.

I speak to your reproductive system in the name of Jesus declaring healing and proper functioning so that within the bounds of holy marriage you may be fruitful and multiply as God intends.

I speak to your integumentary system and declare that your skin, hair, nails, and oil, and sweat glands will function as God intends to protect your body and help regulate temperature and the elimination of waste from your body. I declare all aspects of this system of your body that have been compromised to be healed in Jesus' name.

I speak to your respiratory system consisting of your nose, upper airways and lungs and declare it off-limits to the enemy. I declare that the breath of life God has put within you to sustain you will not be compromised in any way, and all damage to your respiratory system is healed now in the name of Jesus.

I speak to your immune system and command to come into alignment with God's will for your body to act as your physical defense system against all harmful organisms all the days of your life.

I speak to your sleep and say according to proverbs 3:24 You shall no longer lie down in fear and that it is your Father's pleasure to give His beloved sweet sleep as his child. I command a resetting of the sleep center in your brain to experience 6 to 8 hours of uninterrupted sleep every night. I command all nightmares to go, all night tremors to go, night sweats to go, in Jesus' name. I invite God's holy angels to come surround your bed in your bedroom so that your bed is a place of rest and peace, not warfare, in the name of Jesus. I declare sweet dreams over you in the name of Jesus.

By the power of the blood of Jesus Christ I declare you are no longer defined by your history, you are defined by who your God calls you to be. I declare that you are a new creation in Christ. The old has passed away; all things have become new in your life.

This is the 1st day of the rest of your life. Step into your destiny."

New Creation Declaration Blessing

We invite you to make the following new creation declaration over your life.

Look at yourself in the mirror and say this out loud:

"This is who my father says I am, I am a child of the King. I am a co-heir with Jesus. Everything Jesus bought and paid for is my inheritance. I am loved. I am forgiven. I am cleaned by the blood. I am accepted in the Beloved. I am filled with His Spirit. I have angels protecting me and assisting me in the ministry of Jesus. I am United with Jesus. I have been crucified with Christ. I died with Him. I was buried with Him. I was raised with Him. I am seated with Him in the heavenly's far above all rule, all power, all authority and above every name that is named not only at this age but also in the one to come.

Therefore, I carry the authority of Christ. I have the authority over sickness, over sin, over demons and over the world. I am the salt of the Earth. I am the light of the world. All things work together for my good because I love God and I am called according to His purpose, which is for me to be conformed to the image and likeness of Christ. I can do all things to Christ, because greater is He who is in me than he who is in the world."

Appendix B: Declarations

Speak these Declarations of God's Truth over yourself-
Be Encouraged; You Are Loved!

- I am faithful (Ephesians 1:1)
- I am God's child (John 1:12)
- I have been justified (Romans 5:1)
- I am Christ's friend (John 15:15)
- I belong to God (1 Corinthians 6:20)
- I am a member of Christ's Body (1 Corinthians 12:27)
- I am assured all things work together for good (Romans 8:28)
- I have been established, anointed, and sealed by God (2 Corinthians 1:21-22)
- I am confident that God will perfect the work He has begun in me (Philippians 1:6)
- I am a citizen of heaven (Philippians 3:20)
- I am hidden with Christ in God (Colossians 3:3)
- I have not been given a spirit of fear, but of power, love and self-discipline (2 Timothy 1:7)
- I am born of God and the evil one cannot touch me (1 John 5:18)
- I am blessed in the heavenly realms with every spiritual blessing (Ephesians 1:3)

- I am chosen before the creation of the world (Ephesians 1:4, 11)
- I am holy and blameless (Ephesians 1:4)
- I am adopted as his child (Ephesians 1:5)
- I am given God's glorious grace lavishly and without restriction (Ephesians 1:5,8)
- I am in Him (Ephesians 1:7; 1 Corinthians 1:30)
- I have redemption (Ephesians 1:8)
- I am forgiven (Ephesians 1:8; Colossians 1:14)
- I have purpose (Ephesians 1:9 & 3:11)
- I have hope (Ephesians 1:12)
- I am included (Ephesians 1:13)
- I am sealed with the promised Holy Spirit (Ephesians 1:13)
- I am a saint (Ephesians 1:18)
- I am salt and light of the earth (Matthew 5:13-14)
- I have been chosen and God desires me to bear fruit (John 15:1,5)
- I am a personal witness of Jesus Christ (Acts 1:8)
- I am God's coworker (2 Corinthians 6:1)
- I am a minister of reconciliation (2 Corinthians 5:17-20)
- I am alive with Christ (Ephesians 2:5)
- I am raised up with Christ (Ephesians 2:6; Colossians 2:12)
- I am seated with Christ in the heavenly realms (Ephesians 2:6)
- I have been shown the incomparable riches of God's grace (Ephesians 2:7) God has expressed His kindness to me (Ephesians 2:7)
- I am God's workmanship (Ephesians 2:10)
- I have been brought near to God through Christ's blood (Ephesians 2:13)
- I have peace (Ephesians 2:14)
- I have access to the Father (Ephesians 2:18)
- I am a member of God's household (Ephesians 2:19)
- I am secure (Ephesians 2:20)
- I am a holy temple (Ephesians 2:21; 1 Corinthians 6:19)
- I am a dwelling for the Holy Spirit (Ephesians 2:22)

- I share in the promise of Christ Jesus (Ephesians 3:6) God's power works through me (Ephesians 3:7)
- I can approach God with freedom and confidence (Ephesians 3:12)
- I know there is a purpose for my sufferings (Ephesians 3:13) Christ dwells in my heart through faith (Ephesians 3:17)
- I can grasp how wide, long, high and deep Christ's love is (Ephesians 3:18)
- I am completed by God (Ephesians 3:19)
- I can bring glory to God (Ephesians 3:21)
- I have been called (Ephesians 4:1; 2 Timothy 1:9)
- I can be humble, gentle, patient and lovingly tolerant of others (Ephesians 4:2)
- I can mature spiritually (Ephesians 4:15)
- I can be certain of God's truths and the lifestyle which He has called me to (Ephesians 4:17)
- I can have a new attitude and a new lifestyle (Ephesians 4:21-32)
- I can be kind and compassionate to others (Ephesians 4:32)
- I can forgive others (Ephesians 4:32)
- I am a light to others, and can exhibit goodness, righteousness, and truth (Ephesians 5:8-9)
- I can understand what God's will is (Ephesians 5:17)
- I can give thanks for everything (Ephesians 5:20)
- I don't have to always have my own agenda (Ephesians 5:21)
- I can honor God through marriage (Ephesians 5:22-33)
- I can parent my children with composure (Ephesians 6:4)
- I can be strong (Ephesians 6:10)
- I have God's power (Ephesians 6:10)
- I can stand firm in the day of evil (Ephesians 6:13)
- I am dead to sin (Romans 1:12)
- I am not alone (Hebrews 13:5)
- I am growing (Colossians 2:7)
- I am His disciple (John 13:15)
- I am prayed for by Jesus Christ (John 17:20-23)

- I am united with other believers (John 17:20-23)
- I am not in want (Philippians 4:19)
- I possess the mind of Christ (I Corinthians 2:16)
- I am promised eternal life (John 6:47)
- I am promised a full life (John 10:10)
- I am victorious (I John 5:4) My heart and mind are protected with God's peace (Philippians 4:7)
- I am chosen and dearly loved (Colossians 3:12)
- I am blameless (I Corinthians 1:8)
- I am set free (Romans 8:2; John 8:32)
- I am crucified with Christ (Galatians 2:20)
- I am a light in the world (Matthew 5:14)
- I am more than a conqueror (Romans 8:37)
- I am the righteousness of God (2 Corinthians 5:21)
- I am safe (I John 5:18)
- I am part of God's kingdom (Revelation 1:6)
- I am healed from sin (I Peter 2:24)
- I am no longer condemned (Romans 8:1, 2)
- I am not helpless (Philippians 4:13)
- I am overcoming (I John 4:4)
- I am persevering (Philippians 3:14)
- I am protected (John 10:28)
- I am born again (I Peter 1:23)
- I am a new creation (2 Corinthians 5:17)
- I am delivered (Colossians 1:13)
- I am redeemed from the curse of the Law (Galatians 3:13)
- I am qualified to share in His inheritance (Colossians 1:12)
- I am victorious (1 Corinthians 15:57)

Resources

Need Help?

National Human Trafficking Resource Center
1 (888) 373-7888
SMS: 233733 (Text "HELP" or "INFO")
24 hours, 7 days a week
Languages: English, Spanish and 200 more languages
Website: www.traffickingresourcecenter.org

Teen Runaway Help
1-800-RUNAWAY hotline
www.1800runaway.org

24 Hour Prayer Hotline
1-866-273-4444

Substance Abuse
1-800-662-HELP (4357)

National Suicide Prevention Lifeline
Call 1-800-273-8255

Domestic Violence
1-800-799-SAFE

Domestic violence and abuse can happen to anyone, yet the problem is often overlooked, excused, or denied. This is especially true when the abuse is psychological, rather than physical. Verbal Emotional and Mental abuse leave deep scars.
www.ywcasandiego.org/get-help/beckys-house

National Helpline | SAMHSA
Substance Abuse and Mental Health
https://www.samhsa.gov/find-help/national-helpline
Community Resource Hotline: 211
Site: https://211sandiego.communityos.org

Single Mothers Assistance
https://financialassistanceforsinglemothers.com/

Video Links

Drug Dealers Life Transforming Decision

https://youtu.be/nO4NaNjhPTE

Healing from Trauma and PTSD with Dr. Mike Hutchings

https://youtu.be/gxNjCOAvoww

Woman Healed of Trauma by Viewing Healing PTSD Video

https://www.youtube.com/watch?v=Lyb95kaLec8&t=54s

Pulling Down the Stronghold of Fear

https://www.youtube.com/watch?v=FnebJoTO1Fg

Recommended Books

- Supernatural Freedom from the Captivity of Trauma: Dr. Mike Hutchings
- There is More: Dr. Randy Clark
- When Heaven Invades Earth: Dr. Bill Johnson
- The 40 Day Soul Fast: Dr Cindy Trimm
- Without Rival: Lisa Bevere

CPSIA information can be obtained
at www.ICGtesting.com
Printed in the USA
BVHW031654240922
647753BV00007B/27

9 798218 077990